BAIJIU

白酒

BAIJIU
The Essential Guide to Chinese Spirits

DEREK SANDHAUS

VIKING
an imprint of
PENGUIN BOOKS

VIKING

Published by the Penguin Group

Penguin Group (Australia)
707 Collins Street, Melbourne, Victoria 3008, Australia
(a division of Penguin Australia Pty Ltd)

Penguin Group (USA) Inc.
375 Hudson Street, New York, New York 10014, USA

Penguin Group (Canada)
90 Eglinton Avenue East, Suite 700, Toronto, Canada ON M4P 2Y3
(a division of Penguin Canada Books Inc.)

Penguin Books Ltd
80 Strand, London WC2R 0RL, England

Penguin Ireland
25 St Stephen's Green, Dublin 2, Ireland
(a division of Penguin Books Ltd)

Penguin Books India Pvt Ltd
11 Community Centre, Panchsheel Park, New Delhi 110 017, India

Penguin Group (NZ)
67 Apollo Drive, Rosedale, Auckland 0632, New Zealand
(a division of Penguin New Zealand Pty Ltd)

Penguin Books (South Africa) (Pty) Ltd
Rosebank Office Park, Block D, 181 Jan Smuts Avenue, Parktown North, Johannesburg 2196, South Africa

Penguin (Beijing) Ltd
7F, Tower B, Jiaming Center, 27 East Third Ring Road North, Chaoyang District, Beijing 100020, China

Penguin Books Ltd, Registered Offices: 80 Strand, London WC2R 0RL, England

First published by Penguin Group (Australia) in association with Penguin (Beijing) Ltd, 2014

10 9 8 7 6 5 4 3

Text © Derek Sandhaus 2014
The moral right of the author has been asserted

Book design by Steffan Leyshon-Jones © Penguin Group (Australia)
Printed and bound in Singapore by 1010 Printing International Limited

National Library of Australia
Cataloguing-in-Publication data:
Sandhaus, Derek, author.
Baijiu: the essential guide / by Derek Sandhaus.
9780143800132 (paperback)
Alcohol--China--History.
Liquors--China--History.
Distilleries--China.
Distillation--China.
Liquor industry--China.
China--Social life and customs.

641.250951

penguin.com.cn

Derek Sandhaus has published five books on Chinese history and culture, most recently *Drunk in China: Baijiu and the World's Oldest Drinking Culture*. On his journey of 'spiritual' enlightenment, he has met with drinkers, distillers and titans of the Chinese alcohol industry. In 2018 Sandhaus co-founded Ming River Sichuan Baijiu in partnership with China's oldest continually operational distillery. He currently serves as Ming River's baijiu education director and as the editor at DrinkBaijiu.com.

CONTENTS

AUTHOR'S FOREWORD

Almost everything I know about traditional Chinese spirits, or baijiu, I learned the old-fashioned way: one drink at a time. At first I approached my subject with apprehension, which soon gave way to enthusiasm and ultimately admiration. In time, I supplemented this with more methodical research and travel throughout China's major alcohol-producing regions. I have long depended on the kindness of alcohol-wielding strangers, and after several years in which I was particularly blessed in that regard, I have tried to distill my collected findings into this slim volume.

I am not an expert, at least not in the traditional sense, but I have lived the great majority of my adult life in China, a country whose culture and history has always fascinated me. Baijiu can be intimidating to the uninitiated, but it need not always be and I have tried to craft an introduction that is accessible to readers from any background.

This guide is intended to be the book that I wish had existed when I first became interested in baijiu, one that provides context, guidance and clarity as to what baijiu is and what distinguishes it from its global peers. My hope is that you will use it, enjoy it and, most importantly, share what you learn with your friends. If baijiu is destined to become an accepted drink by the world at large, and I believe that it is, baijiu needs not just a diverse audience, but true friends ready to spread the good word. There is a place for baijiu on the shelves of bars around the world (somewhere between the tequila and the slivovitz) and we all have a role to play in helping it get there a little faster.

Derek Sandhaus
Chengdu
September 2013

INTRODUCTION

Few drinks are as widely consumed and misunderstood as baijiu. It is the national drink of China, but has hardly any foreign adherents. To most, it is deadly powerful – exploding on the nose and palate, and packing the alcoholic punch of a prizefighter. One utters its name with the same reverence as when invoking an avenging fury and outsiders who encounter its full might never forget the experience. Baijiu is coming for the world, and the invasion is already well underway.

Baijiu, which literally translates as 'white alcohol', has come to signify a wide range of traditional Chinese spirits that can be as dissimilar from one another as tequila and rum. It is the most popular liquor in China and, by virtue of the population

Mountainous Guizhou Province is revered for its sauce-aroma baijiu

of that great nation, the world. Yet to most drinkers living beyond the Middle Kingdom's borders, Chinese spirits remain a mystery, which is all the more remarkable given their outsized role in daily life.

Alcohol is the lifeblood of Chinese civilisation. Since antiquity, it has shaped and been shaped by the religion and customs of the country. It has inspired the words of poets and the strokes of painters; it has helped forge alliances and exposed enemies; it has lubricated the wheels of business and cemented the bonds of friendship. The wine cup runs over into every facet of China's culture.

The oldest known ding cooking vessel, excavated in Henan near the site of China's earliest alcohols

The 'invention' of alcohol in China predates its recorded history, and possibly even its civilisation. In 1983, archaeologists began unearthing artefacts from the so-called Jiahu civilisation (7000–5800BC) in north-central China's Henan Province. Pottery analysis from the site revealed trace residue of an alcohol made from a mixture of grapes, hawthorn fruit, honey and rice. Not only was it the world's oldest known alcohol, but it was also one of the earliest known instances of rice cultivation for human consumption. The fact that Neolithic Chinese drank alcohol suggests that winemaking may have precipitated the rise of agriculture in China and, as a consequence, civilisation.

This presumption is supported by early written records, which describe alcohol's revered status in ancient times. According to the Confucian classic, *Book of Rites*, it was used to commune with the spirit world by religious and political leaders, and served at important state ceremonies and banquets. Chieftains bequeathed gifts of alcohol to their soldiers to inspire martial valour, and to win over their rivals. The kings of Neolithic China were also no strangers to gross indulgence. Sima Qian's *Records of the Grand Historian* tells of King Zhou of Shang, whose palace contained a manmade lake of wine. The various functions of drink required a steady stream of alcohol, which in turn required an abundance of grain and the development of an elaborate alcoholic bureaucracy.

What set China apart from its global counterparts was that alcohol was always considered a luxury rather than a daily necessity. In early European and Mediterranean civilisations, lack of adequate sanitation made water unsafe to drink and beer and wine became primary sources of clean hydration. Chinese drank boiled water and later tea, which allowed the government greater leeway in the regulation of alcohol. Whether to curb undesirable behaviour or to protect grain stores in times of famine, the government often restricted or prohibited alcohol in antiquity. Taxes and government monopolies on wine production were the preferred method of regulation, which generated tremendous revenues for state coffers and spread the latest brewing techniques to all corners of the empire.

Major Centres of Baijiu Production in China

XINJIANG

TIBET

Legend:

⭐ Capital

◎ Major distillery hubs

PROVINCE

----- Province boundary

＼ Major rivers

----- International border

The first major advancement in Chinese winemaking came around the Han Dynasty (206BC–220AD) with the invention of *jiuqu* or qu. Qu, which lacks a perfect English translation, is essentially a clump of grains that have been mashed and stored in a meticulously controlled environment to cultivate yeasts and other microorganisms. When mixed with the grains used in traditional Chinese alcohols, it converts

starch into sugar and sugar into alcohol. The resulting drink, known as huangjiu or 'yellow alcohol', was a stronger drink than what had preceded and had more complex flavours. Huangjiu production centres developed near early Chinese capitals in the Central Plain – stretching from Shaanxi to Shandong Provinces along the Yellow River – and near the mouth of the Yangtze River in the south.

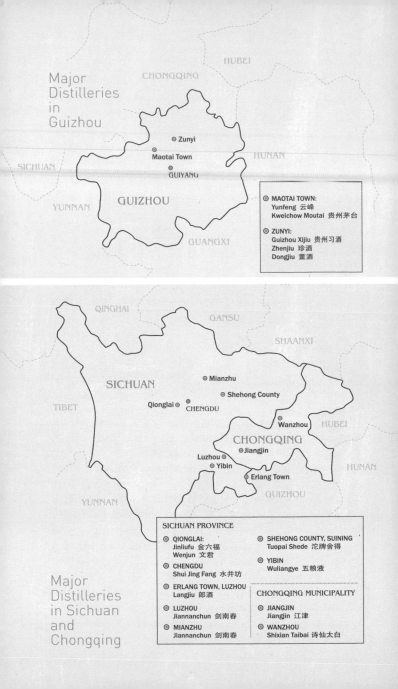

Major
Distilleries
in
Guizhou

HUBEI

CHONGQING

SICHUAN

Zunyi

Maotai Town

GUIYANG

HUNAN

GUIZHOU

YUNNAN

GUANGXI

◎ **MAOTAI TOWN:**
Yunfeng 云峰
Kweichow Moutai 贵州茅台

◎ **ZUNYI:**
Guizhou Xijiu 贵州习酒
Zhenjiu 珍酒
Dongjiu 董酒

QINGHAI

GANSU

SHAANXI

SICHUAN

Mianzhu

Shehong County

Qionglai

CHENGDU

Wanzhou

HUBEI

CHONGQING

TIBET

Luzhou

Jiangjin

Yibin

Erlang Town

HUNAN

YUNNAN

GUIZHOU

SICHUAN PROVINCE

◎ **QIONGLAI:**
Jinliufu 金六福
Wenjun 文君

◎ **CHENGDU**
Shui Jing Fang 水井坊

◎ **ERLANG TOWN, LUZHOU**
Langjiu 郎酒

◎ **LUZHOU**
Jiannanchun 剑南春

◎ **MIANZHU**
Jiannanchun 剑南春

◎ **SHEHONG COUNTY, SUINING**
Tuopai Shede 沱牌舍得

◎ **YIBIN**
Wuliangye 五粮液

CHONGQING MUNICIPALITY

◎ **JIANGJIN**
Jiangjin 江津

◎ **WANZHOU**
Shixian Taibai 诗仙太白

Major
Distilleries
in Sichuan
and
Chongqing

Huangjiu became the favourite alcohol of the elite, its virtues celebrated by poets and scholars.

Distillation, which instigated the second great revolution in Chinese alcohol, arrived much later. Believed to be a foreign invention, the technique by which one turns wine or beer into hard liquor was likely brought to China from the Middle East by either trade during the Song Dynasty (960–1270) or conquest during the Mongolian Yuan Dynasty (1271–1368). The first distilled spirits were probably similar to a brandy or arrack. When this foreign technology was fused with domestic brewing arts, baijiu was born.

In the later dynasties, baijiu became a drink beloved of the farmer and labourer, while huangjiu remained more popular with the scholar-official aristocracy. Spirits were at that time considered less refined than wines, and initial quality standards were low. But huangjiu was expensive and its regular consumption out of the reach of the Chinese peasantry. Baijiu used less grain and was far more potent, and that was precisely what appealed to ordinary people.

Baijiu spread to every province and as it travelled it evolved into several distinct spirits. In the southeast, it took the form of lighter rice spirits. In the rest of the country, Chinese sorghum became the grain of choice. Sorghum was fermented in earthen pits in the southwest and in clay jars in the northeast. Almost every city and village developed its own recipe and techniques, passed down from one generation of distillers to the next.

The past century has witnessed the wholesale transformation of baijiu. Around the fall of the Qing Dynasty in 1912, which marked the end of the imperial system, China began pushing for modernisation and globalisation with a newfound vigour. In 1915, the government sent a delegation of alcohol producers to the Panama-Pacific International Exposition in San Francisco. Several of them, including distillers from Maotai and Xinghuacun, returned home with awards of distinction. Moreover, they returned home with a burgeoning awareness of the Chinese alcohol industry's relative shortcomings and a desire to catch up with their global counterparts. In the decades

The bottling line at **Wuliangye** Distillery in Yibin, Sichuan Province

that followed, Chinese alcohols would compete at several subsequent international and domestic trade fairs to promote the idea of industrialisation and to push forward national Chinese brands. Throughout the country, Chinese entrepreneurs began building China's earliest modern distilleries. But the progress made in the first half of the twentieth century was eventually stalled by foreign invasion and civil war.

Shortly after seizing power in 1949, the Chinese Communist Party embarked on an ambitious plan to nationalise the country's alcohol industry. Production techniques were recorded for the first time, refined to incorporate modern industrial technology, and codified. The government consolidated smaller distilleries into enormous state-run behemoths. Many of China's best-known producers emerged out of this wave of consolidation and industrialisation, including Luzhou Laojiao, Red Star and countless others. Under the government's aegis, baijiu was able to improve its quality and consistency. Most famously, the patronage of long-time Premier Zhou Enlai helped make Kweichow Moutai the Party favourite, and it has been served

at state dinners since the 1950s. With such powerful friends, baijiu finally surpassed huangjiu in prestige.

Chairman Deng Xiaoping's 'Reform and Opening Up' economic policies, which began in the late 1970s, spurred the further expansion of the baijiu industry. The government of Chairman Mao had rationed baijiu, but the drink was now readily available on the market. The reintroduction of private enterprise led to a surge in the formation of new distilleries. In the early 1990s the number of baijiu producers peaked at an estimated 18–36 000. Distilleries invented new baijiu brands, and even new baijiu categories, to capture a greater share of the emerging market. For the first time, people could easily enjoy a variety of spirits produced in distant provinces. This period also saw the advent of up-market baijius, exorbitantly expensive premium and super-premium vanity spirits catering to the newly rich.

The general industry trend in the time since has been towards consolidation and expansion. There are still more than 10 000 distilleries in Mainland China, most of them small to medium-sized regional players, but there exists also a handful

The **Jiuguijiu** Distillery in Xiangxi, Hunan Province, and its celebrated signature baijiu

of distilleries that have created national, and in some cases international, brands. By 2012, an estimated 10 to 17 billion litres (2.6–4.5 billion gallons) of baijiu were being produced annually, a volume more than double that of the nearest global competitor: vodka. That same year, baijiu accounted for as much as two-thirds of the world's ultra-premium spirit sales. Throughout it all, prices skyrocketed, in some cases exceeding several hundred US dollars per bottle.

Shortly after being officially named president in late 2012, China's Xi Jinping announced that the state would withdraw its patronage of the baijiu industry. Many of the nation's leading producers had long relied on massive government orders intended for use at official functions. In 2011, state-run *Global Times* estimated that the Chinese government's food and beverage expenditures exceeded the national defence budget for that year. Xi's policy shift has caused an industry-wide contraction, seeing major producers lower their prices to compete in the crowded consumer market. This has sent ripples through the entire industry, driving down prices of less expensive brands. The heightened competition should also spur innovation and, perhaps more exciting, expansion into foreign markets.

Several Chinese distilleries have begun promoting their products overseas, initially to Chinese expatriates but also increasingly towards local consumers.

At the same time, foreign investment in baijiu is on the rise. Several of the global wine and spirit industry's leading players – Diageo, Pernod Ricard, Louis Vuitton Moët Hennessey and ThaiBev among them – have made forays into the baijiu business with varying degrees of success. Smaller companies around the world have also begun distilling and importing baijiu in the hopes of creating the first truly international baijiu brands.

These are exciting times for the Chinese spirits industry. Like the nation that created it, baijiu has in a matter of decades achieved a level of quality and sophistication that rivals any of its global competitors. It is time that spirits lovers take note. That few have, thus far, can only be attributed to its current obscurity outside of Asia.

This book is intended as a step towards bridging this knowledge gap, but moreover it is a celebration of China's marvellous traditional spirits. The study of baijiu – its various classifications, production techniques and distinctive characteristics – is a worthwhile pursuit for anyone interested in China or its alcohols. But research is no substitute for fieldwork. Those who hope to gain an advanced knowledge of baijiu must imbibe the potent Eastern brew as it was intended, namely in the company of others. To that end, readers will also find brief instructions on Chinese drinking etiquette. Although the specific distilleries and brands included within this collection by no means constitute an exhaustive representation of the tens of thousands of baijius available today, they should serve as a starting point for future connoisseurs.

Baijiu is a spirit unlike anything else, well deserving of a place in the international spirits family. When one drinks baijiu, he or she participates in a tradition that spans more than seven thousand years. While it would be misleading to suggest that one can fully grasp the complexity and depth of the world's most populous nation through its alcohol, this author wholeheartedly commends the attempt. *Ganbei!*

US President Richard Nixon and Chinese Premier Zhou Enlai sharing a historic toast of **Kweichow Moutai** at Beijing's Great Hall of the People in 1972

WHAT MAKES
A SPIRIT CHINESE?

Foreign writing on baijiu tends to focus on its physical character – its faintly industrial bouquet, phenolic sweetness and oesophageal afterburn. While such descriptions are useful in terms of understanding the experience of imbibing Chinese spirits, they fail to capture the extraordinary richness of the category, or to define it.

Chinese spirits are rooted in place, their specific characters highly dependent on local winemaking tradition and the available resources. The chemical processes required to create liquor – fermentation and distillation – are the same in any locale, but the techniques and ingredients used to carry out these reactions are what make Chinese alcohol unique.

Fundamental to the process of making baijiu is the use of solid-state fermentation, which in turn requires solid-state distillation. What this means is that, unlike most Western grain alcohol production such as that of whisky, where yeast is added to sugary liquid broth to induce fermentation, Chinese alcohol is created within a solid mixture of grains. This requires a unique fermentation agent called qu (pronounced the same as the English 'chew') and a host of creative regional fermentation techniques.

In addition to fermentation styles, raw ingredients are also essential. Chinese spirits use several grains seldom found in winemaking outside of Asia and Africa, most notably sorghum, rice and glutinous rice. Water, used in every step of production and generally comprising about half of the finished product, is of critical importance. The availability of a good water source has historically determined the location of China's best baijiu distilleries.

The combination of unique ingredients and techniques creates the flavours and aromas instantly recognisable in Chinese spirits. Subtle distinctions in material and process can produce great variation under the baijiu banner, and a number of sub-categories have emerged. So radical are the differences between baijiu and its Western counterparts, however, that Chinese spirits may rightly be said to represent an entirely distinct school of production.

Baijiu may at first seem unusual, frightening even, to the foreign nose and palate. But the term baijiu denotes so wide a range of liquor that the patient drinker's attempts will invariably be rewarded.

Rice must first be steamed and cooled before the addition of qu triggers saccharification and fermentation

The process of steaming grains prior to fermentation at **Chuangu** Distillery, Sichuan

INGREDIENTS

There's an old saying in Chinese winemaking: 'Water is an alcohol's lifeblood, qu is an alcohol's backbone, and grains are an alcohol's flesh.' In its traditional form, the production of baijiu relies almost entirely upon natural processes and organic raw materials. Which ingredients are selected and the ratios in which they are combined are the single greatest determinants of a baijiu's aroma and flavour.

Water

Water may seem the antithesis of China's fiery liquor, but it is used in every stage of baijiu production. It washes and steams the grain. It adds the moisture that helps trigger fermentation. Its steam passes through the fermented grains during solid-state distillation. After a spirit has been aged, water is again added to dilute the alcohol to the desired strength.

Different types of water produce different results. The minerals within water affect a spirit's flavour and character. Water with low concentrations of minerals, or soft water, is considered a superior solvent and promotes more efficient yeast activity. Water of medium hardness is richer in calcium and magnesium, which increases the acidity of the mash (fermenting grains), breaks down proteins and encourages yeast propagation. Overly hard or acidic water can lead to the formation of solids within the alcohol and corrode equipment, so is typically avoided. Southwestern China, the nation's largest baijiu production

Water from the Li River in northern Guangxi Province is used in the production of several popular rice-based baijius including those of **Guilin Sanhua**

region, tends to have relatively neutral water of medium hardness.

Chinese distillers believe the quality of their water source to be inseparable from the quality of their alcohol, giving rise to the maxim, 'Famous alcohols need outstanding springs.' If a distillery were to relocate, even only slightly upstream, it would alter the alcohol's character. Guilin Sanhua praises the mineral rich water of the Li River and Kweichow Moutai has long celebrated the purity of the Chishui River. So favourable is the Chishui's water that dozens of major distilleries, including several in this book, are situated along its banks, earning it the nickname Meijiu River, or 'River of Beautiful Spirits'.

Many of the best known baijius once drew their water from wells using a traditional Chinese windlass

When fully mature, qu becomes visually saturated with yeasts, molds and bacteria like this brick of big qu

Qu

Qu is the unifying feature of all Chinese wines and spirits. Qu, which turns grains into alcohol, is sometimes incorrectly translated as brewer's yeast, but contains much more than just yeast.

Winemakers produce qu by crushing moistened grains into a paste, forming them into clumps and continuously adjusting their moisture level in a controlled environment. By the end of the process the clumps have drawn yeasts, bacteria and other microorganisms from the air, which coat the surface and interior of the grain clumps. Western alcohol techniques, such as malting, involve sprouting grains to induce saccharification (conversion of starches to sugars) and yeast-induced fermentation (conversion of sugar to alcohol). Chinese winemakers use qu to perform both steps simultaneously.

The predecessor to modern qu was discovered no later than the ancient Zhou Dynasty (1046–256BC), and was likely little more than spoiled grain upon which mould had formed. Chinese brewers refined the technique and developed something resembling modern rice qu by the third century AD. Countless qu recipes exist, but baijiu qu can be divided into two basic categories: big qu and small qu. Big qu generally consists of wheat or barley (and sometimes peas) moulded into large bricks and is the primary fermentation agent for sorghum-based baijiu. Small qu is made from rice, moulded into small balls by hand, and is used as a fermentation agent in most rice-based baijius and huangjius. Sometimes traditional medicinal herbs are added to small qu in order to enhance flavours or impart a therapeutic benefit. Bran qu (*fu qu*) made from the outer membrane of wheat or barley grains, also usually formed into bricks, is another common saccharification and fermentation agent. It is notable for its high alcohol yield, but less complex flavour profiles. Whereas traditional qu relies entirely on air-borne yeast and bacteria, some types of modern qu are inoculated with microorganisms cultivated in the laboratory.

Qu can create subtle differences in taste and recipes are the most carefully guarded secrets in the industry.

Grains

More than any other factor, grains determine the flavour and style of a Chinese alcohol. Grains also provide the starch that will eventually be broken down into alcohol. The most common grains used in Chinese spirits are sorghum and rice, seldom seen in Western alcohol (30 per cent rice-brewed Budweiser being a notable exception). Several other grains play major supporting roles and grain husks, the hard outer layer of certain grains, are key secondary ingredients in Chinese alcohol production, used in a variety of procedures.

Sorghum

The great majority of baijiu is distilled from sorghum, a tough, drought resistant crop from Africa. It probably arrived in central China around 5000 years ago but was not widely used in wine-making until the last millennium. By the early twentieth century as much as 90 per cent of the sorghum grown in southwestern China was used in baijiu production.

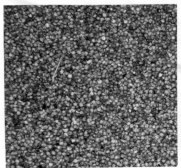

Sorghum is the most widely used grain in baijiu production

Sorghum is grown in tall stalks, somewhat resembling corn or millet in appearance, usually with dark red kernels. As a grain, sorghum is gluten free and high in starch and protein. In wine-making, sorghum has the advantage of easy gelatinisation (the breakdown of starch into a sticky paste) when steamed and does not clump, which can impair fermentation. Sorghum has a bitter taste as a food, because it contains tannins – the compound that gives grape wines astringency. But when distilled, sorghum has a fruity and somewhat nutty fragrance, to which the tannins add desirable complexity of taste.

Baijiu production uses sticky and non-sticky varieties of Chinese sorghum. The non-sticky variety is higher in protein and starch but yields less alcohol than the sticky variety, because the latter more readily absorbs the water necessary for gelatinisation.

Rice

Rice is one of the oldest grains used in Chinese winemaking. Though it is more often used in undistilled alcohols like huangjiu, rice is still the second-most common cereal in baijiu distillation.

Grains of rice have higher starch levels than sorghum but

Rice

contain less protein, fat and fibre. Rice easily absorbs moisture and ferments. When distilled, it retains a pleasant cooked-rice flavour similar to Japanese saké. Rice spirit is slightly yellow in colour and has a crisp, clean aspect on the palate.

Glutinous Rice

Glutinous rice (or sticky rice) imparts a gentle sweetness on spirits. Glutinous rice, like all rice, is actually gluten free and derives its name from its stickiness when steamed, which is why it is sometimes called sticky rice. It has even higher starch levels than its long-grained cousin, which would make it a more desirable raw material if not for its tendency to clump together when cooked. For this reason, glutinous rice is almost always used in combination with other grains for optimal fermentation.

Wheat

Wheat is used as a raw material in complex-grain strong-aroma baijius because of its pleasant, mellow, honey-like notes. More often, though, wheat is used as the primary ingredient for making big qu, the most popular fermentation agent in Chinese baijiu.

Corn

The last of the five primary ingredients used in mixed grain strong-aroma baijiu, corn adds spice and sweetness to the spirit. Corn germ, the grain's embryo, is high in fat and can add oiliness to spirits. It is thus frequently removed prior to use in baijiu distillation.

Other Grains and Starches

Several other grains find their way into baijiu and qu recipes. Buckwheat is sometimes substituted for wheat. Some distilleries ferment other cereals like millet and Job's tears. Barley is used to make certain types of qu. Though not technically a grain, peas are one of the main ingredients in the qu used to make light-aroma baijiu.

Grain husks

Grain Husks

Husks or chaff, the outer shells that enclose certain grains, often go unmentioned on product labels, but they play no small role in the creation of baijiu. Rice husks are by far the most widely used secondary ingredient by Chinese distillers, but millet and sorghum husks are commonly used in northern China, where they are more readily available. The primary function of grain husks is to act as a filler, providing the mash with an additional source of starch and to prevent clumping. The drawback of using husks is that they have an unpleasant taste. Steaming husks can neutralise some of these flavours, but if too many husks are used in the mash it can negatively impact the quality of the baijiu.

Husks also play several minor roles in the production process. Distillers add husks to adjust a mash's starch, acid and moisture levels during fermentation. Husks are also sprinkled on top of fermenting mash as insulation and to mark out distinct layers of mash. Husks are spread on the bottom of Chinese pot stills to prevent mash seepage. Additionally, millet husks are often used as an ingredient in bran qu.

A traditional Chinese thresher, used to separate the husk from grains

风暴机
Hull remover

PRODUCTION OF BAIJIU

For centuries, baijiu was an art passed down from one generation of distillers to the next, but in recent decades it has grown closer to an industrial science. Distillers today use modern equipment. Wheelbarrows have been replaced by cranes; wood and bamboo have been replaced by stainless steel; blending is conducted in a laboratory with beakers and pipettes. Yet for all of this innovation, the fundamentals of baijiu production remain little changed since the Ming Dynasty (1368–1644). Subtle differences of method exist between categories and regions, but the overall flow of production remains the same for all baijius.

The production overviews that follow represent common industry practices rather than official rules. Recipes and techniques often cut across categories.

Preparation of Qu

You cannot make baijiu without qu. This is helpful to remember when considering what qu actually is: a bunch of rotten grain filled with yeasts, moulds and bacteria. But these microorganisms are essential to the process of converting grains into alcohol. Although every factory has its own qu recipe, the two primary types of qu are big qu, used in most sorghum-based baijius, and small qu, used in rice baijius. Both varieties can be made through natural processes, but most modern distillers inoculate their fresh qu with old qu to promote microorganic growth and ensure consistency of flavour.

Baijiu producers cultivate qu in sealed rooms, where conditions are controlled to maximize microorganic growth

Big Qu

Big qu is made principally from wheat or wheat bran, but can also be made from barley, peas and grain husks. It is sub-divided into high- and medium-temperature qu, referring to the heat generated during its incubation period. High-temperature qu can reach temperatures as high as 63°C (145°F), while medium-temperature qu only reaches about 46°C (115°F).

To produce big qu, ingredients are first soaked in warm water for a few hours and then mechanically ground into a coarse powder. Additional water and inoculants are added to the grains, which are then pressed into bricks. The traditional method for making qu bricks is to manually stamp the mixture into a wooden mould with one's feet – a method still employed by some distilleries – but now this can also be accomplished using a machine press, though possibly at the price of valuable fungus. The outer layer of the qu is air dried in sunlight before the bricks are moved to a dark, sealed incubation chamber.

Inside the incubation chamber, qu bricks are stacked on straw mats, leaving small spaces between bricks to encourage

Rice-based small qu

microbial action. The bricks are insulated by straw on all sides, which traps in moisture and regulates temperature. Water is added to the hay in regular intervals if the surrounding climate is warm or dry, and the bricks are flipped weekly. Once the micro-organic infestation begins, the temperature of the bricks rapidly rises. After several weeks, the bricks will dry and cool. The qu will sit in storage for a few months to improve its flavour and is then pulverised into rough particles prior to use.

Small Qu

Small qu is made from rice or glutinous rice flour. The rice is soaked in water for several hours, then mashed into a paste and formed into balls or cakes. The mixture is coated in old qu powder to encourage microbial growth. The qu is placed on a bamboo sieve and moved to a controlled environment for five days to cultivate, then dried and crushed into powder before use.

Traditional Chinese medicine (TCM) is sometimes incorp-orated into small qu recipes. By adding dried herbs (or ginseng, goji berries, deer antlers etc.), winemakers are able to alter a drink's flavours and supposedly endow the spirit with curative properties. During the Ming and Qing Dynasties, this practice was more common and winemakers sometimes included hundreds of ingredients in a single qu recipe. Today small qu is often made with few or no medicinal herbs. Guilin Sanhua, the nation's largest rice baijiu producer, uses only one herb in its qu recipe.

Preparation of Ingredients

There are significant differences in grain preparation depending on the grain and the type of baijiu. The first step often involves grinding kernels into small pieces or powder then adding warm water to remove detritus and increase moisture levels. Grains are steamed to further increase moisture. The key requirements in this stage are that the grain is gelatinised, cooked through and soft. If used, grain husks are steamed separately to eliminate unpleasant flavours. After steaming, the grain is air dried to a temperature that is warm enough to promote microbial growth but not so warm that it will kill the qu's yeasts and bacteria.

Saccharification and Fermentation

Saccharification and fermentation are the two necessary steps required to produce any grain alcohol. Saccharification is the process by which bacteria breaks down starch into sugar. Fermentation is the process by which yeast converts a sugar into carbon dioxide and ethanol (drinking alcohol). Both processes require water and qu. A key distinction of Chinese alcohol is that the grain is always fermented in a solid or semi-solid state.

Distillation

Distillation is the process by which alcohol is converted into steam and cooled back into a more potent liquid, the alcohol's essence or spirit. Because water has a higher boiling temperature than alcohol, if one gradually applies heat to an alcohol, the resulting vapours will at first have much higher alcohol levels than the original liquid. Once the vapours have been captured, they are funnelled into a cooling device that returns it to a liquid state, known as the distillate. Distillates are further subdivided into three categories based on stages of the distillation: in order, the head, heart and tail. The head and tail contain high concentrations of elements either unpleasant or unsafe to consume, so they are typically collected separately. The heart comprises the bulk of what will find its way into the final product.

With the notable exception of some contemporary rice-based spirits, all baijiu is distilled using traditional Chinese pot stills. This device is comprised of two cylindrical barrels – the steamer and the condenser – joined by a tube. The baijiu steamer operates on the same basic principle that applies to bamboo steamers used in dim sum preparation. It consists of a sealable pot, which holds the grains, set atop a cauldron of boiling water separated by a grate to allow steam to rise into the grains. Grain is placed in the pot after the water is brought to a boil. As the temperature of the mash rises, alcoholic vapours will begin to rise from it into the tube where it will travel to the condenser. The condenser is filled with cold water and a pipe leading from the tube to a spigot at its base. The alcoholic vapours will pass through the tube, cooled by the water back into alcohol, and begin flowing out the spigot into a waiting receptacle. The head and tail are cut, and the tail is sometimes redistilled to remove impurities, and preserved.

Fresh distillate from the still is usually collected in stainless steel containers

A cross-section of a traditional Chinese still

Steamed grains are often spread on the ground to cool prior to fermentation

Sealed fermentation pits at the **Wuliangye** Distillery

Modern Chinese pot stills

The **Xiaoerbulake** Distillery in Xinjiang Province aging its products outside

The steaming of grains prior to fermentation is also conducted in the still's steamer. When making types of baijiu that require multiple cycles of fermentation and distillation, freshly added grains are sometimes added to the mash and steamed in concert with distillation before more qu is added and fermentation begins anew. Less desirable distillate is sometimes poured into a mash prior to fermentation in order to improve flavour and raise a mash's acidity. Each round of distillate is collected and stored separately.

Aging

Baijiu producers consider a freshly produced distillate, known as *yuanjiu* or 'original spirit', an incomplete product until it has been aged. Aging baijiu smoothes the rough edges of a raw spirit, reducing its harshness while imparting more complex and

Most baijiu is aged in cool, dark places protected from sunlight, most commonly in a cellar. **Guchuan** stores some of its best baijiu in jars buried directly in the ground

rounded flavours. Most baijiu is matured at least six months and premium baijiu distillers typically age their spirits for at least three to five years.

The basic principles governing the aging of Western spirits apply equally to baijiu. Fresh distillate contains certain undesirable elements, aldehyde foremost among them, which give the spirit an astringent taste and irritate the throat and larynx. Storing a spirit in a carefully controlled environment allows it to interact with oxygen, which breaks down aldehyde and improves the concentration of esters. These esters give the alcohol a sweeter flavour and more complex aroma. Because the interactions are gradual, the alcohol will continue to develop as long as it is aged. However, as time passes, some of the alcohol will evaporate – what is known in the Western alcohol world as the 'angel's share'.

What distinguishes traditional Chinese alcohol aging from its Western counterparts is the exclusive use of clay aging vessels. (The ancient Mediterraneans fermented and aged their wine in clay amphorae and dolia, but the technique was lost.) The decomposition of rocks produces clay, so its mineral composition varies according to region. When fired into aging vessels, the

Guilin Sanhua ages its premium baijiu in the Elephant Trunk Hill cellar in downtown Guilin alongside the Li River

clay forms a porous surface that facilitates oxidisation. Additionally, the minerals that comprise the clay interact with the alcohol to improve its flavour. Simply put, clay aging helps diminish the negative aspects of baijiu while imparting more desirable aromas and flavours.

As aging depends heavily on an alcohol's interaction with its environment, storage conditions are critical. Moisture in the air can reduce alcohol evaporation and dilute strength, but dry storage conditions have the opposite effect. Most consider the optimal conditions for aging baijiu to be in a temperate and humid setting protected from the elements. Many baijiu distillers age their products in dank subterranean cellars or in cliff-side caves. The Guilin Sanhua Distillery, to take a prominent example, ages its products in Elephant Trunk Hill, one of the limestone formations for which Guilin is famous.

Despite the benefits of aging, consumers should note that China currently has no national standards for the labelling of aged products. Bottles claiming to contain a particularly old spirit – anything predating the baijiu boom of the 1990s – may be younger than advertised or contain only the slightest trace of an aged baijiu in its blend.

Blending

Blending is what distinguishes a distillery's top-shelf baijiu from its more common offerings. Because all baijiu is fermented in batches, there is often great disparity in the relative quality and flavour of each mash, and also within the various production stages of an individual mash. When varieties of baijiu employ multiple stages of fermentation and distillation, the distillate collected at every step will be stored and aged separately. The job of a baijiu master blender is to create a finished product from the various aged distillates that best harmonises their respective flavours and aromas. Consistency is critical: A blender must be able to replicate a brand's characteristic flavour and make necessary adjustments to compensate for changing conditions within the distillery.

In general, most of the blend will be composed of the lighter flavours that come from the heart (the distillate, that is). The more intense, lingering flavours produced towards the tail will then be added in moderation to provide complexity. It is not

Blending is integral to creating exceptional baijiu

The bottling plant at **Kweichow Moutai**

uncommon for more reputable baijiu distilleries to purchase inexpensive aged distillate, or even neutral spirits (ethanol), from obscure distilleries to incorporate into its low-to-mid-range blends. Although this practice is common in blended whiskies and perfectly harmless to consumers, it has caused controversy among baijiu purists, as distilleries are not legally required to disclose the use of third-party distillate and seldom do.

Purified water is added to the blend to bring down the alcohol level. Often the same blend will be bottled at various strengths – usually between 36–65% ABV – to appeal to different consumers. Following blending, the finished product is stored in stainless steel vats to coalesce and await bottling.

Bottles of **Kweichow Moutai** being prepared for packaging

The sorghum used in sauce-aroma baijiu is
fermented in pits lined with stone bricks

TYPES OF BAIJIU

Though often discussed as if it were a single type of spirit, baijiu is a tree with many branches. In terms of ingredients, production methods and flavours, baijius can be worlds apart. Baijiu is divided into four primary categories by smell – strong, light, sauce and rice aroma – and a handful of smaller, often brand-specific categories. The current classification system is a modern innovation and not without its limitations, but it is a useful reference point for any drinker. Though baijiu styles have historically been linked to specific regions, geographic lines have begun to blur in recent decades and new flavours are continuing to emerge.

Luzhou Laojiao ferments its grains in mud pits, the oldest of which date from 1573

The **Kweichow Moutai** Distillery in Guizhou Province

Primary Aromas

Strong Aroma

Nong Xiang
浓香

Easily the most popular and widely produced category of baijiu, strong-aroma baijiu is fermented in earthen pits. There are two variations of strong-aroma baijiu: simple grain (*danliang* 单粮) and mixed grain (*zaliang* 杂粮), respectively distilled from one or more grains. In taste, strong aroma is fiery with a fruity sweetness. Strong aroma has intimate regional ties to Sichuan in the south-west, China's largest alcohol producing province, as well as the eastern provinces of Anhui, Jiangsu and Shandong.

Light Aroma

Qing Xiang
清香

The second-biggest category by volume, light-aroma baijiu is distilled from sorghum and rice husks fermented in stone jars and pits. Light-aroma is divided into two sub-categories: erguotou 二锅头 ('second pot head', originally from Beijing) and Fenjiu 汾酒 ('Fen' spirit, named for the city from which it derives: Fenyang, Shanxi Province). Light-aroma baijiu is fermented with big qu made from barley and peas, and typically has a mild floral sweetness. It is commonly associated with northern China.

Sauce Aroma

Jiang Xiang
酱香

Sauce-aroma baijiu derives its name from its distinct and lingering fragrance, which is said to resemble soy sauce. It is a mellow spirit, with a layered taste of herbs and fermented beans, and a long aftertaste. Sauce-aroma production is labour and resource intensive, involving multiple fermentations in subterranean pits lined with stone bricks. The category is most closely associated with southeastern Sichuan and northwestern Guizhou, specifically the township of Maotai and the Kweichow Moutai Distillery.

Rice Aroma

Mi Xiang
米香

Rice-aroma baijiu is most closely related to huangjiu in its production methods. It is distilled from long-grain rice, glutinous rice or a combination of the two and fermented with small rice qu, often containing Chinese medicinal herbs. Rice-aroma baijiu is aged in limestone caves, and often infused with fruits, herbs, tea flowers or TCM. At its best, rice aroma is smooth and mild, resembling Japanese saké in taste. Rice baijiu is produced throughout southern China, but is most closely linked to Guangxi and Guangdong provinces in the southeast.

Other Aromas

Phoenix Aroma

Feng Xiang
凤香

Named after Xifengjiu, 'West Phoenix Spirit', from Fengxiang County, Shaanxi Province, phoenix aroma combines aspects of the strong- and light-aroma categories. It is distilled primarily from sorghum fermented in earthen pits with a wheat, barley and pea-based qu. Unlike strong-aroma baijiu, phoenix-aroma producers replace the mud lining its fermentation pits each year and employ a short ten-day fermentation period. Following distillation, phoenix-aroma baijiu is aged in the 'seas of alcohol': giant rattan baskets filled with cloth sacks hardened with vegetable oil, beeswax and pig's blood. These baijius are notable for their fruity aromas, grainy taste and expanding finishes.

Mixed Aroma

Jian Xiang
兼香

Mixed aroma is less a distinct category than a combination of categories. A mixed aroma baijiu is produced by combining production techniques or blends from two different baijiu categories. The most common mixed aromas are hybrids of strong and sauce aromas, either of which may play the predominant role.

Chi Aroma

Chi Xiang
豉香

Invented in Guangdong Province in 1895 by what later became the Shiwan Distillery, chi aroma's name refers to *douchi*, a salty Chinese condiment made from fermented beans. Chi aroma is indistinguishable from rice-aroma baijiu in all respects save one: It is aged with an infusion of pork fat. Accordingly, this unkosher variety is sometimes called fat aroma (*zhi xiang* 脂香) and has an oily body with subtle bacon overtones.

Sesame Aroma

Zhima Xiang
芝麻香

Jingzhi Distillery in Shandong first produced sesame aroma in 1957. It is made primarily from sorghum with wheat qu, and also sometimes millet and barley. Fermentation is carried out in a stone-lined pit with a mud bottom, developing distinct flavours depending on depth and position in the pit. Sesame aroma is a close relative of sauce-aroma baijiu but is fermented at higher temperatures for a shorter amount of time, and thus has a more charred, nutty flavour.

Medicine Aroma

Yao Xiang
药香

Dongjiu Distillery of Guizhou pioneered medicine-aroma baijiu, also known as Dong aroma (董香, which rather begs for a better translation). Using a sorghum base, the alcohol is fermented in two pits, the larger pit performs fermentation using big qu and the smaller pit uses rice qu filled with Chinese medicinal herbs. The pits are lined with high-alkaline white mud mixed with wild peach juice and sealed with coal. After extraction from the pit, the two mashes are mixed together and distilled. Medicine aroma is a layered liquor that marries sweet and savoury flavours.

Extra-Strong Aroma

Fuyu Xiang
馥郁香

Extra-strong aroma is associated with Hunan's Jiuguijiu Distillery. It is distilled from sorghum and glutinous rice fermented with big qu and small medicinal qu, and aged for at least three years. It has a pungent earthy fragrance and a spicy-sweet taste. According to master blender Madame Wu Xiaoping, who coined the category's name, mixed-aroma baijius combine aspects of two baijiu categories, while extra-strong aroma combines at least three. (Note: *Fuyu xiang* literally translates as 'strong-aroma aroma', but to avoid confusion the extra-strong label has been chosen to reflect the category's complexity.)

Special Aroma

Te Xiang
特香

Named after its producer, Jiangxi's Sitir (also *Si Te* or 'Four Specials') Distillery, special aroma is fermented from rice and big qu in pits of red stone bricks joined with cement and sealed with mud. Its fragrance is earthy, but its taste is light with a rich, slightly tart aftertaste.

Lao-baigan Aroma

Laobaigan Xiang
老白干香

Hengshui Ruitian Distillery's laobaigan baijiu is similar to erguotou light-aroma baijiu in almost every respect. It uses wheat qu but is also aged for a shorter period of time than light-aroma, typically no more than six months. Usually bottled at over 65% ABV, it has a fruity flavour overshadowed by a searing alcoholic flame.

Small-Qu Baijiu

Xiao Qu Baijiu
小曲白酒

Another hybrid, small-qu baijiu (also small-qu light-aroma baijiu) is primarily distilled from sorghum and fermented in pots with rice qu. It retains light aroma's mild floral character, but also contains some of the mellowness of rice aroma.

The original **Shui Jing Fang** Distillery in Chengdu, Sichuan Province, was built upon the ruins of a recently excavated workshop that dates back to the Ming Dynasty

STRONG-AROMA BAIJIU
浓香

Ingredients: Simple grain – Sorghum;
mixed grain - sorghum, rice, glutinous rice, corn and wheat
Qu: Wheat
Leading brands: Wuliangye, Luzhou Laojiao, Jiannanchun

Strong-aroma baijiu production places special emphasis on maintaining continuity between batches and minimising waste. Its defining characteristic is the use of mud fermentation pits, which continually absorb microorganisms from the qu and develop sophisticated flavours over the course of decades and, in some instances, centuries. Another distinction is its use of a continuous mash (or 'ten thousand-year mash'), in which a previously distilled mash is recycled with the addition of fresh grains and qu. Mixing spent mash with the fresh grains increases the resulting mixture's acidity, improving the aroma and helping to break down starches and proteins. The so-called 'thousand-year pit, ten-thousand-year mash' marries a pit and mash in an endless cycle to ensure maximum yield of alcohol and continuity of flavour.

The production process begins with the end of the previous fermentation cycle. Fermentation pits are unloaded a layer at a time and distilled in separate batches. The surface mash, roughly a quarter of a pit's mash, contains the least amount of alcohol and is sold as livestock feed after it has been distilled. An amount of crushed fresh grain equivalent to the volume of the discarded spent mash is added to the remaining distilled mash – called the 'mother mash' – and stirred together. About ten to fifteen minutes later, when the fresh grains have had the chance to absorb some of the moisture from the mother mash, rice bran is stirred in quickly to limit alcohol evaporation, just long enough to evenly distribute the fresh ingredients.

Following distillation of the previous pit's surface mash, the water in the steamer is replaced and the mother mash-fresh grain mixture is loaded evenly into the steamer and distilled for about an hour, discarding the head, setting aside the heart and retaining the tail for a second distillation. The steamer is then unloaded and hot water is poured onto the grains to increase the moisture level for fermentation and further gelatinise the fresh grains while inhibiting bacterial growth. The grains are then spread onto the cooling ground to lower the temperature to a suitable level for adding qu.

Once qu has been added to the mash and the bottom of the pit, the mash is loaded back into the pit. After each batch is deposited, the mash is levelled and stomped down to reduce aeration. A layer of rice husks is often laid between the surface mash and the lower mash to demarcate layers. Once the surface mash is level with the ground, rice husks are sprinkled on top as insulation and a layer of mud at least 30 centimetres high is applied to seal the pit and keep out airborne microorganisms that might affect fermentation. The seal is regularly moistened to prevent the mud from drying and cracking, and covered with plastic if it becomes too dry. As the grains ferment, they lose resilience and the mud seal sinks into the pit. Once the seal has descended enough, in about two to three months' time, the grains are ready for distillation and the cycle begins anew.

The distillate from various batches can vary greatly in terms of quality, taste and smell, and are aged separately for at least six months before blending and bottling. The lowest level of pit mash contains the highest amount of alcohol and consequently produces the most prized baijiu. Most premium strong-aroma baijiu brands age their products for at least one to three years in ceramic or stainless steel pots.

LIGHT-AROMA BAIJIU
清 香

Ingredients: Sorghum, rice husks
Qu: Barley and peas; wheat bran
Leading brands: Xinghuacun Fenjiu, Red Star, Niulanshan

A milder alternative to other sorghum-based baijius, light aroma refers to the taste and smell, not strength – light aroma is frequently bottled at upwards of 65% ABV. Light aroma is principally produced and consumed in northern China and Taiwan. From a production standpoint, the defining characteristic of light-aroma baijiu is a short production cycle and, in its traditional form, the use of stone pots as fermentation vessels.

Light aromas may be subdivided into two main sub-categories: Fenjiu and erguotou. Fenjiu, named for Fenyang in Shanxi Province, is an aromatic and complex pot-fermented spirit, popular at the mid-range level. Erguotou, formerly known as 'The Burning Dagger', is the more economical baijiu of Beijing, sold for next to nothing at any Chinese convenience store. Erguotou is less expensive due to its frequent use of higher-yield fermentation vessels (stone or steel pits), inexpensive ingredients (often fermented with bran qu and blended with neutral spirits), and short fermentation cycles.

Sorghum kernels for light aroma are gently smashed into four to eight pieces. Hot water is poured onto grains, evenly mixed and formed into piles. The piles are stirred two to three times over the course of a day, during which the grain absorbs the water.

The sorghum used in Fenjiu style baijiu is fermented in earthenware pots set into the ground and sealed with stone

The grains are loaded into the pot and steamed until cooked through but not so long that they become sticky and clump together. Immediately after removing from the steamer, cool water is poured onto the grains, which are then air-dried. Once the temperature of the grains has dropped enough, qu is added and stirred into the steamed sorghum.

The sorgum is loaded into the fermentation vessel. In the case of Fenjiu, this is a clay pot, approximately a meter in depth and diameter. These pots are placed in holes in the ground so that their lips are level with the surface. A heavy stone lid is placed atop the jar and the edges are plugged tight with grain husks. An additional layer of husks or straw is scattered atop the sealed jars to maintain a consistent fermentation temperature. For Fenjiu, the fermentation period is about three to four weeks; for erguotou, four to eight days. Following fermentation, the mash is removed from the jar and slowly sprinkled into the steamer for distillation.

Fenjiu employs a second fermentation and distillation to maximise the alcohol yield. After the first fermentation rice husks are added to the mash at a ratio of one to four and steamed during the first distillation. The mash is cooled after distillation, fresh qu is added and the second fermentation and distillation are performed. The distillate from each cycle is stored separately.

The distillate is aged in ceramic jars for at least one to three years for Fenjiu, and six to twelve months for erguotou.

SAUCE-AROMA BAIJIU
醬 香

Ingredients: Sorghum
Qu: Wheat
Leading brands: Kweichow Moutai, Langjiu

Sauce-aroma baijiu production is characterised by repetition with slight variation. Fermented and distilled in eight cycles, it requires a significant investment in grain, labour and time – a full production cycle lasts about a year, aging withstanding. Unique to the category is the use of the piling saccharification-fermentation technique and fermentation pits lined with stone bricks.

When selecting sorghum for sauce-aroma, only about a quarter of the kernels should be pulverised, the rest is left whole or in large pieces. The sorghum is washed several times in warm water to remove detritus and allow the sorghum to absorb liquid. It is then steamed for about two hours and spread on the ground to cool, being turned over with shovels throughout.

Once the sorghum has cooled to the desired temperature, qu is added and the mixture is formed into mounds of approximately two meters in height. Piling the mash helps to saccharify the grain while absorbing some of the microorganisms present in the surrounding air. Over the course of a couple days, fermentation begins and microorganic clusters will become visible on the mound in white patches. The temperature of the mound will gradually rise and a fruity smell will begin to emanate.

Stills at the **Kweichow Moutai** Distillery

When the distiller determines by touch that a mound has achieved the required core temperature, the mash is shovelled into the fermentation pits. The pits are sealed with mud to prevent aeration and left to continue fermenting. After a month, the seals are removed and the mash is mixed with freshly washed sorghum in equal parts, and distilled. The mash is spread to cool, and sprinkled with qu and some of the distillate. The fermentation process is repeated, from piling to pit, fresh grains are added for the last time and a second distillation is conducted, this time reserving the distillate. Every month the mash goes through another fermentation-distillation cycle until the seventh and final distillation, roughly nine months into the production process. The distillate produced in each cycle has different chemical characteristics, alcohol levels and flavours: The liquor from early cycles is harsh and sour, while the middle cycles are smooth and aromatic, and the last cycles are bitter and smoky.

The various distillates are aged separately for at least three years in ceramic urns and blended together to achieve a balanced flavour. The final product is typically bottled at 53% ABV.

RICE-AROMA BAIJIU
米香

Ingredients: Rice, glutinous rice
Qu: Rice, medicinal herbs
Leading brands: Guilin Sanhua, Kiukiang

Rice baijiu is the pride of southeastern China and traces its roots back to the region's ancient rice wines. A perfect union of technological innovation and natural bounty, rice aroma brings together modern distillation technology and the lush local terrain. Out of all the major categories, rice-aroma baijiu makes the best case for being in a class of its own. In terms of production, it is more closely related to huangjiu, particularly transparent rice wine (*mijiu*), than other categories of baijiu; their production processes are virtually identical up to the point of distillation. In taste, it has the sweet crispness of a Japanese saké with pleasing floral notes and an aroma so mild it is hard to recognise as a baijiu.

The rice used in rice-aroma baijiu is washed for an hour in warm water to remove detritus and begin breaking down the grain's exterior. Rice is then dried and steamed three times to ensure optimal gelatinisation. Once cooked, the rice is cooled by fans.

After small-qu powder has been added to the rice, the mixture is stirred together and moved to a squat stone jar. A hole is dug in the centre of the rice to allow for aeration and a bamboo cover is placed atop the jar to await saccharification. After about a day, the grains are moved to a larger capacity jar. Water is added to trigger fermentation and the rice is left to ferment for five or six days.

Rice fermenting at **Guilin Sanhua** Distillery

Traditionally, rice-aroma baijiu has been distilled in Chinese pot stills like the other aroma categories, but in recent years some of the major producers have begun using modern continuous stills, which produce a smoother but less flavourful final product similar to vodka. For this reason, rice-aroma baijiu is the only category that regularly performs distillation in a liquid state better suited to multiple distillations. After discarding the head and the tail, the resulting distillate is around 58% ABV and has a light yellowish colour.

Rice-aroma baijiu is aged for at least one year in ceramic jars, often stored in limestone caves.

Rice is saccharified in small jars before it is moved into a larger jar for fermentation

Unlike those in other categories, some rice-aroma baijius employ continuous stills to achieve a milder character

Drinking Chinese alcohol is mercifully free from pretension. In China today, there exists no real culture of connoisseurship when it comes to traditional drinks and little concern for maintaining a respectable veneer once the bottle opens. As soon as the baijiu begins to flow, one should consider the invitation extended and whatever inebriation follows as an acceptable consequence.

Though the drinking culture is casual, drinking etiquette is strict. No matter how raucous the drinking may get in the Middle Kingdom – and it can get quite rowdy – the consumption of alcohol is guided by an elaborate set of protocol whose origins are as ancient as China itself. These customs govern everything from where one sits to when one drinks.

Setting

There is a popular saying in China, 'You can't set the table without wine', which is to say that you cannot hold a feast at which alcohol is absent. Alcohol is always served with meals, the basic unit of Chinese social exchange. The connection between Chinese cuisine and alcohol runs deep: Not only is alcohol used in the preparation of several classic dishes, but it also draws out and accentuates the flavours of regional cooking (most experts recommend pairing baijiu with the distillery's special regional dishes, a convenient and intuitive rule). This means that baijiu is most often found at restaurants, banquet halls or the family

Yuan in Shanghai is one of several bars in China that have begun to distinguish themselves by serving original baijiu cocktails

dinner table, and rarely at modern nightlife venues like bars, clubs and karaoke parlours.

Chinese drinking rituals are rooted in hospitality customs and reflect the respective roles of host and guest. As Chinese banquet tables are typically round, the host or guest with the most seniority is expected to sit in the seat with the most direct line of sight to the door. Other guests are expected to position themselves on the host's flanks in descending status. If one is unsure of where to sit, it is recommended to wait for the host to indicate a place.

When pouring alcohol, one never fills one's own glass unless individual baijiu carafes have been provided. Pours should be generous, full to overflowing, in order to make each guest feel welcome. The recipient indicates his respect to the pourer by lightly tapping the table with one finger as a symbolic kowtow.

This tradition supposedly hearkens back to the times of Emperor Qianlong, who sometimes poured tea for his entourage while travelling incognito, a gross breach of court etiquette. His subjects would perform the mock-kowtow finger tap to demonstrate their fealty to the Emperor without revealing his true identity.

When serving baijiu in a traditional glass, it is important to fill to the brim

Toasting

A drinking session commences with the host's toast, usually thanking guests for attending, wishing them happiness and good fortune, and inviting them to enjoy the meal. All guests raise their glasses, clink with other guests (if the table is too large, tapping one's glass against the lazy Susan found at the centre of most banquet tables is also acceptable), then drinking deeply from the glass.

Following the initial toast, all attendees are free to toast whomever they like. When clinking glasses, one is supposed to keep the lip of one's glass below that of a drinker of higher standing. In practice, most participants will try to prostrate themselves before the other, and the toast devolves into a comic race to the tabletop.

In northern China, baijiu is served in glasses the size of a teacup, and the quantity consumed with each toast is at the discretion of the drinker. In the south, it is more popular to drink out of small, thimble-sized shot glasses, drained in full with each toast to a loud shout of '*Ganbei!*' or 'Dry the glass!' Following each *ganbei*-style toast, both drinkers hold up their emptied glasses for the inspection of the other.

Baijiu is often infused with traditional Chinese medicine like ginseng, goji berries and snakes

Aside from toasts, little baijiu is consumed at a meal – casual drinking is typically reserved for beer, wine or soft drinks – but since custom dictates each toast imparted must be returned in kind, the amount of alcohol consumed can escalate quickly. It is common for several bottles to be consumed in one sitting. Obviously such immoderate consumption is laden with risk, to one's health and dignity, so it is important to pace oneself, drink plenty of water and lay down a good base of food when engaged in a *ganbei* free-for-all. In extreme cases, one may need to risk offense and refrain from further drinking.

Infusing and Mixing

Aside from its use as an intoxicating social and professional lubricant, alcohol is most commonly used in Chinese culture as a health tonic. For thousands of years, Chinese have steeped their drinks with traditional herbs, medicines and animal parts to impart a curative or revitalising effect. There are countless recipes, but common ingredients include ginseng, goji berries and snakes, as well as deer antlers and testicles. Although the initial object of creating these concoctions was to neutralise

Private stores of baijiu aging at the **Guchuan** Distillery in Qionglai, Sichuan Province

the bitter taste of traditional Chinese medicines, some herbs and spices can mellow the harsh edge of a baijiu and improve its flavour. China also boasts many delicious traditional fruit infusions, such as plum wine, consumed for non-holistic purposes.

A more modern invention is the baijiu cocktail. Though not the traditional method of consumption, baijiu cocktails are beginning to appear on drink lists around the world. Purists frown upon anything that masks the aroma or strength of a Chinese spirit, but baijiu cocktails offer bartenders a wide array of exciting new tastes with which to experiment. Moreover, baijiu distillers are eager to see their products embraced by a younger and more cosmopolitan audience, and a good cocktail may be the perfect delivery system for taking baijiu from Chinese restaurants into the bars and clubs of the world.

Shui Jing Fang Scholar's Edition is a limited edition product intended for gifting

Gifting

The practice of giving gifts to improve relationships and show respect is widespread in China. Gifting – so-called because it sounds better than bribery – is one of the primary drivers of the super-premium baijiu market. With such gifts, one intends to impress the recipient with the bottle's quality, so going with a well-known brand is recommended over something more obscure. In general, the more

expensive the bottle, the better the gift. If an outrageously priced baijiu is not an option, a solid mid-range bottle will do in a pinch. Do not, under any circumstance, give a low-end baijiu as a gift. It would be preferable to give no gift at all. In one notorious historical incident, Duke Gong of Lu presented bad wine to King Xuan of Chu, kicking off a war that inadvertently almost ended the Zhao Kingdom.

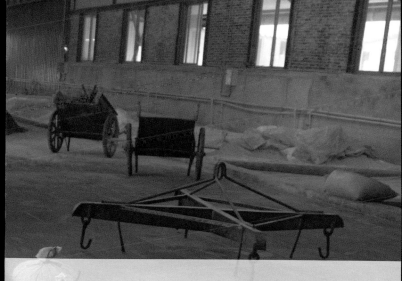

BAIJIUS

白酒

BAIJIU: THE ESSENTIAL GUIDE TO CHINESE SPIRITS

Hong Kong Baijiu
Strong Aroma
43% ABV
Ingredients: Sorghum, rice, glutinous rice, wheat, corn

Hong Kong Baijiu has a delicate bouquet of green apples and meadow grass on the nose, with notes of hawthorn and toffee on the tongue.

Many foreigners had their first taste of Chinese alcohol in the former British colony of Hong Kong, yet the city has never been a modern centre of baijiu production. Thus 500 Spirits' Hong Kong Baijiu (HKB) pays homage not to the spirits of Hong Kong but the spirit of Hong Kong – its harmonious fusion of Eastern and Western ideals.

Parisian entrepreneur Charles Lanthier first developed a taste for baijiu while working and living for several years in the Chinese mainland. Wanting to share his passion with the world, he established 500 Spirits in 2013 and launched HKB the following year with an eye towards high-end cocktail bars. Distilled in Sichuan, tweaked for Western tastes in Europe, and sold into the North American market, it is a truly international baijiu.

Baishaye
白沙液
Mixed Aroma
52% ABV
Ingredients: Sorghum, wheat, glutinous rice

Baishaye has the mellow nose and finish of a sauce aroma, but the intense fiery sweetness of a strong aroma. Its bottle is intended to look like a traditional drinking gourd.

BAIJIUS

Founded in 1952 as the Changsha Distillery, what is now Baisha began producing mixed-aroma baijiu in the 1970s, making it one of the category's originators. It remains a relatively small-scale distillery today, only producing several thousand tonnes of baijiu annually, but does not want for patriotic bona fides. In 1974 Mao Zedong, Hunan's favourite son, made a visit that coincided with his birthday. When a local official toasted his health, the Chairman asked what he was drinking. 'Just some no-name baijiu from the Changsha Distillery,' came the reply. Declaring it a superior liquor brewed with the waters of the old Baisha Well, Mao told them it should be called Baisha Liquid (Baisha Ye). And when the Great Helmsman made a birthday request (or any request, really), there was only one correct answer.

BAIYUNBIAN 白云边
Songzi, Hubei | www.hbbyb.com

Wuxing
五星
Mixed Aroma
42% ABV
Ingredients: Sorghum

The smooth and gentle Wuxing or 'Five Star' baijiu has a minty, floral aroma and a short finish. Some tasters note a hint of toasted rice on the nose.

Hubei's Baiyunbian, founded in 1952, is a leading representative of the mixed-aroma category. Its name comes from a verse by Li Bai, China's most celebrated drunk, in which the immortal poet gazes at a Hubei lake and imagines riding his boat into the night sky and drinking 'beside the white clouds' or *baiyun bian*. In 1974, Baiyunbian became one of the first distilleries to experiment with complex production techniques that incorporate elements of strong- and sauce-aroma categories. Its silver medal showing at the government's 1979 National Alcohol Appraisal launched a wave of regional imitators. Not to be outdone, Baiyunbian literally set the standard for the category by subsequently publishing the national guidelines for mixed-aroma baijiu production. The company currently operates multiple distilleries in Hubei and Sichuan.

Guojing
国井
Sesame Aroma
46% ABV
Ingredients: Sorghum, wheat, rice, glutinous rice, corn, barley millet

Guojing or 'National Well' has notes of fermented soybean and sesame oil balanced with a strong estery sweetness that verges on phenolic.

BAIJIUS

This baijiu takes its name from Bandao Well in Gaoqing. According to legend, the exhausted troops of tenth century general Zhao Kuangyin found the well after an arduous retreat, but could not retrieve water from its depths. Zhao's prayers were answered when the well miraculously bubbled over, restoring his army and paving the way for a successful conquest. Zhao would go on to found the Song Dynasty as Emperor Taizu.

The Gaoqing Distillery began operations in 1957, mostly as a producer of ethanol for industrial use. In 1980 it started distilling solid-state baijiu, and established the Bandaojing Company nineteen years later. Determined not to lose the mixed-grain arms race, Bandaojing uses a seven-grain blend in its flagship product.

BAOFENG 宝丰

Baofeng County, Pingdingshan, Henan | www.hnbfjy.com

Guose
国色
Light Aroma
52% ABV
Ingredients: Sorghum

Guose or 'National Colour', uses a qu recipe that includes wheat, barley and peas to create an understated spirit with a bitter, strongly alcoholic finish.

In Chinese, Baofeng means 'rich in treasure', a name the place has well deserved, owing to an archaeological bounty that spans back to the Neolithic Age. The earliest records of Chinese alcohol suggest that a female cook named Yi Di first invented alcohol for mythic Emperor Yu the Great, and locals believe she crafted her wines at Baofeng. By the Song Dynasty (960–1279), Baofeng winemaking had developed to such heights that the empire studied its methods for dissemination to remote provinces. In 1948 Baofeng County established Henan's first modern distillery, Yuchangyuan, whose name was changed to Baofeng Distillery in 1956. Its production techniques are rooted in neither the Fenjiu nor the erguotou schools, making it one of the most distinct iterations in the light-aroma class.

Rouhe 5 Year
柔和 5 年
Sauce Aroma
45% ABV
Ingredients: Sorghum

Rouhe smells faintly of canta-
loupe. It hits the palate hard,
mellows to sweetness in the
middle and has a lingering taste
of liquorice towards the end.

The so-called 'Moutai of the North', Manchurian favourite
Beidacang got its start a century ago as Qiqihar's celebrated
Juyuanyong Distillery. It survived the ravages of the early
twentieth century northern warlords and the rise and fall of
the Japanese puppet state Manchukuo, but was ultimately
nationalised as the Qiqihar Distillery in 1951. The northwest is
known for light-aroma baijiu, but Beidacang was one of the first
distilleries to buck the trend. Its distillers studied sauce-aroma
baijiu in Moutai prior to the Chinese Civil War, and made five
subsequent educational trips thereafter. The end result was
the creation of the far northeast's first sauce-aroma baijiu. In
1981, the distillery changed its name to Beidacang or 'Northern
Breadbasket' after its flagship liquor.

**Yongfeng Erguotou
10 Year**
永丰二锅头十年
Light Aroma
50% ABV
Ingredients: Sorghum

This simple yet assertive baijiu has a mild aroma and a savoury taste that becomes slightly bitter. A typical erguotou with a hot, clean finish.

During the height of the Chinese Civil War, the People's Liberation Army suffered heavy casualties in its northeastern campaigns. Battlefield medicine required sterilisers and anti-septics, so the northern army decided to establish the makeshift 'Prosperity Springs' erguotou distillery at Renqiu, Hebei, which could supply both needs. In 1949, when the PLA liberated Beijing, the Communists expelled the owners of Daxing District's Yuxing Distillery, which had once served the imperial court of the Qing Dynasty, and replaced it with the transplanted Renqiu factory. The new Daxing Distillery later changed its name to the Beijing Erguotou Distillery, and established itself as a leading mid-level producer of erguotou with an annual production capacity of more than 10,000 tonnes. In recent years Beijing Erguotou has also started releasing strong-aroma baijius.

Red
Light Aroma
40% ABV
Ingredients: Sorghum

An easily approachable baijiu with notes of pineapple and grain in the nose and melon and apple on the palate. The finish is short, sweet and smooth.

Houston-born Matt Trusch first visited China as a language student in 1988 and it was love at first sight. The next two decades saw him bounce around the country, first to Harbin, then Beijing and ultimately Shanghai. Along the way he studied, worked in various industries and cultivated a journeyman's appreciation for sorghum spirits. He decided to share his passion with the world and, in 2006, shortly before returning home, Trusch and his wife created a business plan for Byejoe, 'Chinese liquor with a Western twist'.

Under the guidance of managing director Silvio Leal, a seasoned alcohol industry executive who had overseen product launches for Seagram's and Moët Hennessey, Byejoe saw a way forward along vodka and tequila's inroads. As team Byejoe sees it, the chief hurdles that baijiu needs to overcome for the Western »

Dragon Fire
Infused Light Aroma
35% ABV
Ingredients: Sorghum, dragon fruit, lychee, hot peppers

Made from the same base baijiu as Red, Dragon Fire has a strong lychee aroma with no trace of alcoholic bite. On the tongue, the lychee sweetness melts into a peppery spiciness on the tongue.

market are the four Ps: proof, pungency, purity and price-tag (or, to transpose the formula four letters: strength, smell, safety and savings). To this end, Byejoe developed an East-meets-West spirit, authentically Chinese but attuned to Western sensibilities.

Byejoe's Red series, a lower-alcohol baijiu for the North American market, was launched in 2013. Using a light-aroma base distilled in Maotai Town, Byejoe blends, filters and bottles its spirits in the United States. Byejoe's bottle design won a Double Gold award at the 2013 San Francisco World Spirits Competition, where it also outperformed Kweichow Moutai in tasting evaluations. Later that year, Byejoe launched Dragon Fire, the first infused international baijiu. Byejoe's products are currently the only Chinese spirits officially certified in the United States as gluten-free and kosher.

Changleshao 5 Year
长乐烧五年窖藏
Rice Aroma
54% ABV
Ingredients: Rice

Changleshao gives off a whiff of apricot and flowers, but the initial sweetness quickly gives way to a searing short-lived finish.

BAIJIUS

One of the many theories for how ancient Chinese rice wine first arrived from the Central Plain and found an enduring home in the far south, was that it was introduced by the Hakka. Though the Hakka's origins are mysterious, they represent a unique Chinese cultural strain in Southeast Asia replete with their own language, customs and winemaking techniques. In eastern Guangdong's Meizhou, the Hakka have been brewing *mijiu*, a clear saccharine rice wine, for more than a thousand years. Back then Wuhua County was called Changle, and when distilled spirits or *shaojiu* arrived in later dynasties, the area adapted its traditional wine to the new technology. The Changleshao Distillery split off from the Wuhua County Distillery in 1978 and was purchased by the Ruihua Corporation in 2000.

Teniang
特酿
Strong Aroma
45% ABV
Ingredients: Sorghum, rice, glutinous rice, wheat, corn

A well-balanced baijiu with aromas of cooked rice and bean paste. Has a lingering spicy-sweet finish that one normally associates with pricier brands.

Although Qionglai's history as a bulk baijiu production centre has stained its reputation in the eyes of some baijiu experts, many of its native distilleries like Chuangu produce spirits worthy of national attention. Wang Jianqiang, current owner of Chuangu Distillery, is the thirteenth lineal descendent of the Wang Distillery, founded in the seventeenth century. A stone relief discovered near the site of the modern Chuangu Distillery and dating from the mid-nineteenth century bears an inscription from the town mayor who lavishes praise upon the Wang Distillery for its excellent spirits and philanthropic work in the community. The current iteration of the distillery started in 2009 and primarily sells its own brands in China's east coast markets. In addition to baijiu production, Chuangu also breeds deer for use in medicinal tonics.

Danmi
丹米
Rice Aroma
38% ABV
Ingredients: Rice

At 38% ABV, this is the strongest of the series, which also includes 28% and 22%. This is still an exceptionally mild baijiu that smells of rice husks and pear.

BAIJIUS

Danquan, formerly the state-owned Nandan County Distillery, was established in 1956 and has expanded rapidly since the start of this century. The distillery is situated in a lush, mountainous region in northeastern Guangxi, along the border with Guizhou. Despite being firmly in rice-aroma country, Danquan is just a short distance from the centres of sauce- and strong-aroma baijius in Guizhou and Sichuan Provinces. Its diverse range of products reflects this situation: At present Danquan's stated annual output is 20 000 tonnes of rice aroma, 10 000 tonnes of strong aroma, and 6 000 tonnes of sauce aroma. Most of its products are sold within Guangxi Province.

Laolingchuan 3 Year
老陵川三年窖
Mixed Aroma
38% ABV
Ingredients: Sorghum, Job's tears, rice

Has an unusual aroma, like a freshly sharpened pencil and beeswax. A smooth, savoury baijiu with no trace of alcoholic bite in the finish.

While the Lingchuan Distillery was moving out of its old factory in 1996, it discovered the ruins of an ancient, fully-stocked baijiu cellar. The aging vessels within were giant wooden casks with a capacity of 4 tonnes each, lined with a hardened paper sheath and containing an imperial court wine dating from 1845, twenty-fifth year of Emperor Daoguang (*Daoguang Nianwu*) by ancient reckoning.

Its signature Lingchuan baijiu is only produced using traditional Manchu distilling techniques, fermenting atypical local grains with TCM and aging in wooden 'seas of alcohol' plastered with deer's blood. In 1954, Zhu De, supreme commander of the People's Liberation Army, wrote, 'The south has Moutai, the north has Lingchuan.'

Guomi
国 密
Medicine Aroma
54% ABV
Ingredients: Sorghum

Guomi literally translates as 'State Secret'. Behind its musty, cheesy nose hides an intense burst of flavours including fruit, liquorice, white pepper and brine. There's nothing else quite like it.

BAIJIUS

The lone medicine-aroma baijiu, Dongjiu is shrouded in affected secrecy. Its name comes from the Donggongsi Temple in northern Zunyi, a suburb that became a hotbed for winemaking in the seventeenth century. The local technique was wholly distinct from that of nearby Maotai, but was almost lost in the early years of Communist rule. In 1957, the government revitalised the industry by building the Dongjiu Distillery. Sorghum is fermented in big pits with big qu and in small pits with small qu, which are then combined before distillation. Dongjiu coats its pits with white mud, lime and star fruit stems, and seals them with coal. Notably, the distillery adds more than a hundred medicinal herbs to its small qu. Dongjiu's complex recipe has supposedly been named a national secret: Visitors are allowed inside the factory, but pictures are strictly forbidden.

Confucius Wisdom: A Wise Man's Spirit

儒 家 智 慧

Strong Aroma

39% ABV

Ingredients: Sorghum

A soft, gentle spirit with a muted aroma and pleasant fruitiness. Well suited to the baijiu novitiate, but just strong enough for the seasoned drinker.

Everest Spirits' Confucius Wisdom bills itself as a 'wise man's spirit', and though time will ultimately determine the wisdom of bringing baijiu to foreign shores, one cannot help but admire the attempt. Beijing-born David W. Zhou left behind a career in corporate IT to found Everest Spirits when he failed to find a single bottle of baijiu anywhere in the Washington, D.C. metropolitan area outside of Chinatown. Zhou singled out two primary factors for baijiu's past inability to establish a foothold in Western markets – the price and the alcohol level were both too high – and created a product that addressed both concerns. Confucius Wisdom launched in 2012 and hopes to put forward the best face of Chinese culture, albeit in liquid form, and won double gold at the 2014 World Beverage Competition. Everest Spirits distills and bottles entirely in China.

Danya Yinzhuang
淡雅银装
Strong Aroma
42% ABV

Ingredients: Sorghum, rice, wheat, glutinous rice, corn

A basic but highly drinkable strong aroma. It's just potent enough to provide a little kick but not strong enough to drown out the layered fruity flavours.

Qionglai, roughly 50 miles west of Chengdu, is China's most important centre for *yuanjiu* – raw alcohol intended for blending and bottling – and Guchuan sits at the head of the Qionglai Distillers' Association. A private company founded in 1994, Guchuan is an all-purpose supplier: Its five local distilleries specialise in strong-aroma baijiu, but also produce sauce and light aromas. Its success has prompted it to begin selling its own brands on the market. In 2010 the company broke ground on a new production complex in Qionglai's rapidly expanding baijiu development zone (near the new factories of Shui Jing Fang, Jinliufu and other notables), which will expand its total annual production capacity to 10000 tonnes by 2015. Also, in 2010, Guchuan purchased the Toudao Distillery in Jilin Province, renaming it Bainian Helong.

BAIJIUS

GUILIN SANHUA 桂林三花

Xiangshan Dongcang
象山洞藏
Rice Aroma
52% ABV
Ingredients: Rice

From the Elephant Trunk Hill reserve, this offering has a mild nose with notes of grass and lemon. A dry and bitter spirit with a hot finish and pronounced rice flavour.

Guilin Sanhua is the reigning king of rice baijiu. The twin southeastern provinces of Guangxi and Guangdong have been producing rice wines for as long as records have been kept. Guilin Sanhua rice spirits are first mentioned in a list of the empire's greatest alcohols during the Ming Dynasty (1368–1644). The popularity of rice baijiu spread quickly throughout the region, as products were shipped downstream from the then provincial capital at Guilin along the Li River to future rice baijiu powerhouses like Foshan and Guangdong.

Smelling the floral aromas of *sanhua jiu* or 'three flower spirits', one might mistakenly conclude that its name is intended in a literal sense, but Guilin Sanhua's origins are as complex as the spirit itself. In local alcoholic parlance, alcohol 'flowers' are bubbles, and the ancient method of determining

Laoguilin
老桂林
Rice Aroma
45% ABV
Ingredients: Glutinous rice, rice

One of the most interesting modern baijius on the market, Lao Guilin has a yeasty aroma, a muted spiciness, and a slightly vanilla taste. Its medium finish evokes rose essence.

an alcohol's strength was to observe the bubble patterns formed within the drink when it was jostled. The surface tension of the best types of alcohol would result in the formation of three distinct clusters of bubbles. Another theory, championed by the south China layman, is that the three flowers refer to the production methods. In the creation of traditional rice baijiu, the rice is thrice steamed before qu is added. Rice-aroma baijiu is sometimes distilled as many as three times in a pot still – in early foreign accounts of drinking baijiu in Guangdong, it is called *samshu* or 'triple distilled'.

Today, Guilin Sanhua Distillery neither counts bubbles nor triple distils – it uses column stills that perform many more distillations. It has instead re-appropriated the three 'flowers' to represent the natural bounty of northern Guangxi: the waters »

Sanhuajiu 10 Year
三花酒 10 洞藏
Rice Aroma
52% ABV
Ingredients: Rice

Smells of toasted rice and sweet pear. This is a well-balanced spirit with marshmallow notes and an easy, medium finish.

of the Li River used for brewing, the rice that is distilled, and the traditional herbs mixed into its qu. This harmony of industry and environment is further emphasised by the use of the region's celebrated karst (limestone hills) as aging cellars. All of Guilin Sanhua's top-level spirits are aged in a two-story, 3000-square-metre cellar inside Elephant Trunk Hill, situated alongside the Li River in the heart of Guilin.

Guilin Sanhua Distillery was formally established from the conglomeration of several private distilleries in 1952. It currently produces 20000 tonnes annually, most of which is inexpensive liquor often used as a base for herbal infusions.

**Xiangshan Laotan
8 Year**

湘山老坛8年

Rice Aroma

50% ABV

Ingredients: Rice

Laotan, or 'Old Jar', has a citrusy bouquet that balances well with its understated flavours of cooked rice, roasted barley and orange peel.

BAIJIUS

The Guangxi Quanzhou Xiangshan Distillery was established in 1954 at the convergence of the Xiang and Guan Rivers in northern Guilin. It takes its name from the Quanzhou County's Buddhist Xiangshan Temple. Originally Xiangshan exclusively produced rice wines according to local traditions, but began improving its quality with the introduction of modern qu-making techniques in the early 1960s. In addition to rice-aroma baijiu distilled in the traditional Guangxi style, Xiangshan also produces rice wines and medicinal tonics, with a combined annual production level of 25 000 tonnes. Hong Kong-based alcohol conglomerate VATS Group purchased the distillery in 2008 and changed its name to the present form.

Jinzhi
金质
Sauce Aroma
53% ABV
Ingredients: Sorghum

Jinzhi's rich, creamy fragrance gives way to a nutty, herbaceous flavour with a prickly finish. A smooth and mellow spirit.

Established in 1952 along the banks of the Chishui River, The Guizhou Xijiu Distillery benefits from the same natural conditions that have created so many exceptional sauce-aroma baijius in northwestern Guizhou. Guizhou Xijiu made headlines in 2012 when Xi Jinping, whose surname is represented by the same Chinese character used in the distillery's name, was officially appointed China's next president. Long-time Party darling Moutai, which had purchased the distillery in 1988, sensed an opportunity to once more ride political currents to material gain. During the 18th National Congress, where delegates elected presumptive nominee Xi, media was awash with Guizhou advertisements. Unfortunately President Xi disappointed the distillery's expectations by reining in official spending on boozy banquets within months of assuming office.

Gujinggongjiu Nianfen Yuanjiang

古 井 贡 酒 年 份 原 浆

Strong Aroma

50% ABV

Ingredients: Sorghum, rice, glutinous rice, wheat, corn

An exceedingly smooth and gentle strong aroma. A hot front-end with notes of jasmine rice and marshmallow give way to a liquorice finish.

BAIJIUS

Bozhou-native Cao Cao – statesman, poet, warlord, and the fictionalised arch-villain of the *Romance of the Three Kingdoms* – explained the art of winemaking to the last Han Dynasty emperor in 196AD. It remains the oldest surviving Chinese wine recipe and Cao Cao's alcoholic legacy lives on in Gujinggongjiu, sometimes called 'Cao Cao liquor', a key ingredient in local specialty Cao Cao chicken (not to be confused with the chicken favoured by a later General Cao). By the late imperial era, the alcohol brewed with water from a thousand-year-old ancient well in Bozhou's Jiandian Village was considered the 'flower of the Huai River spirits'. In 1959, Jiandian's state-run distillery changed its name to Gujing and began producing its nationally famous Gujinggongjiu or 'Old Well Tribute Wine'.

Hengshui Laobaigan
衡水老白干
Laobaigan
67% ABV
Ingredients: Sorghum

Though it smells faintly of banana, whatever taste laobaigan – pronounced laobai *garr* in the northern patois – might have is quickly sucked into a flaming alcoholic vortex. Adding a splash of water is advised.

Hengshui's ancient Taocheng District has been making potent spirits for as long as anyone remembers, giving rise to the expression, 'When you open its wine jars, the smell travels ten miles and makes a thousand homes drunk.' During the Ming Dynasty, a flourishing spirits industry sprung up around Taocheng's Hengshui Bridge. Using the waters of the Fuyang River, they created a sweet yet searing spirit, strong enough to shift mountains. In most respects similar to Beijing's erguotou-style baijiu, the Hengshui style ferments with different qu and a much shorter production cycle. By the sixteenth century, it was already called laobaigan or 'old, white, dry' in reference to its ancient origins, purity and extremely high alcohol content (no water added). In 1946, the eighteen surviving laobaigan producers were combined to form Hengshui Ruitian Distillery.

Yuanjiang
原浆
Small-Qu Baijiu
52% ABV
Ingredients: Sorghum

A mild floral aroma and a light, crisp, somewhat herby body. Derives nice marshmallowy undertones from the rice qu. A very well made low-end baijiu.

Small-qu baijiu is Sichuan's best kept secret. Inexpensive, clean and mild, small qu (sometimes styled small-qu light aroma) lends itself equally well to infusions and *ganbeis*. With an annual production capacity of 30 000 tonnes, nobody makes more small qu than Jiangjin Distillery. Just southwest of down-town Chongqing along the banks of the Yangtze, Jiangjin was already an established Sichuanese liquor producer by the early twentieth century (Chongqing was part of Sichuan until 1997). It was said that one could smell the alcohol from miles away. Hongmei Distillery, the most famous of the bunch, was nationalised in 1951 and ultimately renamed Jiangjin County Distillery. Its first factory manager, Fan Zhihong, developed the brewing techniques still used today. His book *Fan Clan Brewing Techniques* laid the groundwork for others in the category.

BAIJIUS

BAIJIU: THE ESSENTIAL GUIDE TO CHINESE SPIRITS

Jian Nan Chun Chiew
剑南春酒
Strong Aroma
52% ABV
Ingredients: Sorghum, rice, glutinous rice, wheat and corn

Jiannanchun's flagship baijiu emits a subtle, floral and somewhat nutty aroma that belies its ferocity on the palate. It has a strong yet balanced taste of pineapple and pepper, and goes down cleanly.

In chronicling the finest wines of the empire, ninth century writer Li Zhao singles out the burnt wine from Sichuan's South of the Sword region (*Jiannan zhi Shaochun*). While the ancient tipple is only tenuously connected to the Jiannanchun of today, the Mianzhu-based distillery still has an impressive historic pedigree. During the Song Dynasty (960–1269), Mianzhu was already celebrated for its honey wine and 'light yellow' wine, a huangjiu made from sorghum, glutinous rice and wheat. By the early eighteenth century, the city had gained esteem for its big-qu baijiu and boasted dozens of regionally famous producers. One of the larger and more famous distilleries, Tianyi Laohao, contained seven units with twenty-six fermentation pits (the distillery has been well preserved and is now a protected cultural heritage site).

Mianzhu Daqu
绵 竹 大 曲
Strong Aroma
52% ABV

Ingredients: Sorghum, rice, glutinous rice, wheat and corn

Still one of the bestselling low-end strong aromas, this series has a milder fragrance but a harsher finish than the more expensive brands.

The story of modern Jiannanchun begins with the creation of the Mianzhu Daqu brand in the early twentieth century. The product was intended to promote the city's baijiu at the provincial and regional level, and it was chosen as the name for a state-run distillery founded from the consolidation of Mianzhu distilleries in 1951. In 1958, the government sent an industry group to review the production techniques of the Mianzhu Daqu Distillery. On the visitors' suggestion, the distillery modified its recipe, abandoning its sorghum-only spirits for ones that also included rice, glutinous rice, wheat and corn. The new recipe was a more complex blend that hearkened back to the light yellow wine of ages past, and is still one of the leading low-end strong-aroma baijius. That same year the distillery formally changed its name to Jiannanchun. »

Dongfanghong
东方红
Strong Aroma
46% ABV
Ingredients: Sorghum, rice, glutinous rice, wheat and corn

A significant upgrade in price and quality from Jian Nan Chun Chiew, Dongfanghong ('The East is Red') has a pronounced chrysanthemum nose, a layered apricot-like flavour and a gentle character.

Jiannanchun has been a privately owned business since 1998, and has since been a shrewd player in the domestic and international baijiu markets. In 2001, Jiannanchun purchased the ailing Qionglai-based Wenjun Distillery, rehabilitated the brand, and sold a majority stake to LVMH (Louis Vuitton Moët Hennessey) in 2006. That same year, it entered into a joint-venture with Swedish alcohol giant V&S (itself later acquired by Pernod Ricard) to create a new high-end brand, Tianchengxiang. Meanwhile, the company's flagship Jian Nan Chun Chiew became one of the best-selling premium baijiu brands in the nation.

Tragedy struck in 2008, when an 8.0-magnitude earthquake erupted in Beichuan and killed over 68000 people in surrounding regions. Nearby Mianzhu was the second-worst hit city.

Tianchengxiang
天 成 祥

Mixed Aroma
52% ABV

Ingredients: Sorghum, rice, glutinous rice, wheat and corn

The child of the joint venture between Jiannanchun and V&S/Pernod Ricard, Tianchengxiang is an 80 per cent strong aroma, 20 per cent sauce aroma crowd-pleaser with a full-bodied and earthy taste.

Jiannanchun Distillery was badly damaged – almost 40 per cent of its aged liquor was destroyed and the company suffered total losses in excess of RMB1 billion (then about US$140 million).

Jiannanchun has proved resilient since the disaster. Although it no longer holds the same lofty number-three sales position in national sales it had before 2008, the company has been quick to rebuild and continues to offer consistently high-quality premium baijiu at more reasonable prices than its chief strong-aroma competitors.

JINGZHI 景芝

Jingzhi Town, Anqiu, Shandong | www.jingyangchun.com

Yipin Jingzhi
一品景芝
Sesame Aroma
38% ABV
Ingredients: Sorghum, rice, glutinous rice, wheat, corn

This classic sesame-aroma baijiu smells faintly of soy, but is much nuttier than its sauce-aroma cousins. Also sold in higher strengths.

Shandong's Jingzhi Town has been making alcohol as long as anyone. Archaeologists have unearthed prehistoric alcohol vessels there dating back at least 4 500 years, and stone reliefs from the Han Dynasty detailing every stage of the ancient brewing process. In later dynasties, local distillers crafted Jingzhi Gaoshao, later Jingzhi Baigan, the north's most famous *gaoliang* according to a 1920 journal. In 1948, the Red Army took control of Jingzhi and thereupon merged seventy-two private spirits workshops into the Jingzhi Distillery. Though the distillery continues to produce Jingzhi Baigan, today it is the standard-bearer of sesame-aroma baijiu, which it invented in 1957, and became an officially recognised category in 1984. That same year, Jingzhi altered its recipe to become a five-grain baijiu. Its annual production capacity is 60 000 tonnes.

Xijiu
喜 酒
Strong Aroma
52% ABV

Ingredients: Sorghum, rice, glutinous rice, wheat, corn

Emblazoned with the double-happiness symbol, Xijiu is a characteristic red bottle intended for wedding banquets. It is a sweet but herby baijiu with hints of fermented bean.

BAIJIUS

Yibin's Wuliangye created the Jinliufu brand as an inexpensive banquet baijiu in 1998, but the so-called 'prosperity spirit' has become a modern, brand-driven company in its own right. It was an official sponsor of the 2002 Chinese National Men's Soccer Team (the only team to ever qualify for the World Cup) and the 2008 Beijing Olympics, and it regularly releases special edition bottles for national holidays and traditional celebrations. Perhaps more notable than Jinliufu's baijiu are the activities of its subsidiary. Beijing-based VATS Group, which has acquired over a dozen wine and spirits producers including one of Qionglai's biggest distilleries, China Zhongheng Huchung, in 2005. Two years later it broke ground on a vast modern Qionglai distillery at a cost of RMB250 million (US$41 million), with an annual production capacity of more than 30000 tonnes.

Jiuguijiu
酒鬼酒
Extra-Strong Aroma
52% ABV
Ingredients: Sorghum, rice, glutinous rice, wheat, corn

Jiuguijiu has the pungency of a blue cheese, a clean finish and a layered flavour that contains a little bit of everything: fruit, stinky tofu, nuts, liquorice, roasted herbs and juniper.

Like other central Chinese distilleries, Jiuguijiu makes up for its historical paucity with boundless creativity. Its name refers to a line of poetry by Hunan artist Huang Yongyu: 'The drunkard becomes the drunken immortal'. Founded in 1956, Jiuguijiu or 'Drunkard's Liquor' was the result of a calculated government innovation drive in 1979.

Jiuguijiu became a publicly-listed corporation with several subsidiary businesses in 1997, and promptly established itself as a pioneer in baijiu marketing. In 2005, the Hunan Provincial Science and Technology Department officially recognised Jiuguijiu's blend of big- and small-qu styles as a new category of baijiu: extra-strong aroma. Two years later, Jiuguijiu relaunched with a new recipe developed by leading national master blender Madame Wu Xiaoping of Guojiao 1573 and Wenjun fame.

Kinmen Kaoliang 58
金门高粱 58
Light Aroma
58% ABV
Ingredients: Sorghum

The classic Taiwanese *gaoliang*, also available at 38% ABV. A round and flavourful spirit with a lingering finish. Smells of musty grain and chamomile.

BAIJIUS

Kinmen Kaoliang, foremost among Taiwanese *gaoliang* baijiu, is one of the few happy accidents of the Chinese Civil War. Charged with the defence of Kinmen Island, which is adjacent to Fujian Province, Kuomintang General Hu Lien twice repelled Communist assaults in 1949 and 1958. In between engagements, he instituted a policy of planting sorghum to boost the local economy. In 1952, Lien's subordinates established the Nine Dragons River Distillery, exchanging rice for sorghum pound-for-pound with the local farmers. In 1956, the remains of the Nationalist Government in Fujian fled to Kinmen, where it took charge of operations and renamed the distillery after the island. Kinmen has employed traditional north China distilling methods since its inception, and ages its high-end products in the underground tunnel networks of former military installations.

KIUKIANG 九江

Foshan, Guangdong | www.kiukiang.com

Kiukiang Shuang Zheng Chiew

九江双蒸酒

Chi Aroma

29.5% ABV

Ingredients: Rice

Double-distilled and laced with swine, this is an oily spirit with herbal flavours. Don't let the alcohol level fool you, it still packs a wallop.

Kiukiang's company slogan is *'yuanhang'*, meaning 'voyage to faraway lands by boat', which suits the seafaring people of southwest China. But it may be more fitting than they realise. The state founded the distillery in 1952 through the merger of twelve private distilleries, some of which had hundreds of years of history. The distillery specialises in pork-fat infused rice baijiu, and its signature products are double- and triple-distilled baijiu. The latter spirit gained notoriety among the early Western sailors in Guangdong under the name *samshu* (Cantonese for 'thrice fired'). *Samshu* caused not a small amount of mischief in the nineteenth century, earning itself an official ban from the admiralty. The effects of one particularly disastrous *samshu*-induced brawl may have been responsible for kicking off the First Opium War in 1839.

Kouzijiao 6 Year
口子窖6年
Mixed Aroma
41% ABV
Ingredients: Sorghum, rice, wheat

Made using a wheat-barley-pea qu and a mixed-grain mash, this is an easily approachable baijiu with prominent notes of rice and fermented bean.

BAIJIUS

Suixi County locals like to say, 'One cannot hide Kouzi from people'. Kouzi baijiu's aroma is so sharp and penetrating that the bottle cannot contain it. In earlier times Kouzi bottles were encased in bamboo sheaths and the fragrance supposedly rose from the basket. It used to be said that when shipments of Kouzi arrived at the Nanjing docks, the scent enveloped the entire city. It's even known as a 'morning after-aroma' baijiu, because of how its taste lingers in a drinker's mouth.

The modern Kouzi Distillery was established in 1997 from the merger of the Huaibei Kouzi and Suixi County Kouzi Distilleries. It sits on the eastern banks of the Sui River, where the original Kouzi distilleries were located. Traditionally a strong-aroma distillery, Kouzi's Kouzijiao mixed-aroma series is its most popular contemporary offering.

Feitian
飞天
Sauce Aroma
53% ABV
Ingredients: Sorghum

Feitian or 'Flying Fairy', is Moutai's flagship brand. Its fragrance recalls dark soy sauce and fermented grains, and a nutty, somewhat bitter herbal taste. It is sometimes bottled as Wuxing or 'Five Star' for official channels.

Popularly known as the 'National Liquor', Moutai is not only the most famous baijiu distillery in China, but the only well-known Chinese liquor abroad. Moutai is served at all high-level Chinese state dinners and is frequently given as a gift by Chinese foreign delegations. Personages no less than Ho Chi Minh, Kim Il-Sung, Richard Nixon and Barack Obama have drunk Moutai with Chinese dignitaries. So important is Moutai to Chinese diplomacy that Henry Kissinger once famously remarked to then-president Deng Xiaoping, 'I think if we drink enough Moutai, we can solve anything.'

Standard half-litre bottles of its signature Flying Fairy brand have at times sold for prices more than US$300, and vintage bottles have sold at auction for hundreds of thousands. Central to the question of Moutai's inordinate success is how Maotai,

Kweichow Moutai
贵州茅台

Sauce Aroma

53% ABV

Ingredients: Sorghum

A special edition luxury product, this is a truly exquisite baijiu. Amid the usual sauce-aroma flavours are rich notes of dark chocolate, coffee grounds and walnut.

a remote village in Guizhou, one of China's poorest and most inaccessible provinces, has produced China's most coveted baijiu. The answer is in part historic caprice.

Guizhou is an ethnically diverse region, and though most Chinese minorities produce their own traditional wines, it failed to produce spirits whose quality was comparable to nearby Sichuan. During the Qing Dynasty (1644–1911), the state instituted a salt monopoly with Maotai as a distribution hub. Northern merchants stationed there were so dissatisfied with the state of Maotai's spirits that they imported the best distillers from their home provinces to merge the latest distillation techniques with local traditions. The result was an alcohol called *huisha*, or 'native soil', that became exceptionally fragrant when aged. It was the forerunner to modern Moutai liquor. »

Prince
王子
Sauce Aroma
53% ABV
Ingredients: Sorghum

A step down from Flying Fairy, Prince is a mid-level baijiu with a prominent light soy nose and fiery finish.

But in China business is all about connections, particularly government connections, and Moutai strikes all the right patriotic notes. During the war-torn decades of the early twentieth century, Moutai became a favourite among the troops of the warlords. During Mao Zedong's Long March, the Red Army passed Maotai's Chishui ('Red Water') River four times, using the local baijiu to boost morale and disinfect wounds. After the revolution had succeeded, so many of the new nation's leaders were already enamoured of it that its success was assured.

The Kweichow Moutai Distillery was established in 1951 through the amalgamation of several local spirits producers, and under the patronage of Premier Zhou Enlai, Moutai became the preferred official banquet liquor of the Chinese Communist Party. In the 1970s, Zhou went a step further by protecting

Yingbin
迎宾
Sauce Aroma
53% ABV
Ingredients: Sorghum

Another mid-level offering, Yingbin is somewhat tart, with a light nutty taste and a mild finish.

the Chishui River from pollution by banning upstream industry, thus ensuring a clean source of water for future Moutai distillers. The Chishui, which now boasts dozens of additional distilleries, is also called the Meijiu River or 'River of Beautiful Spirits'.

As the original sauce-aroma baijiu, Moutai has spawned countless imitators and fakers and remains the nation's most valuable liquor brand. In 2004, Moutai reached an exclusive duty-free distribution agreement with Camus Cognac. At the 2012 World-Spirits Award, Moutai's Small Batch took home a gold medal, the first major international award earned by a modern baijiu and in 2013, *Forbes* magazine named Moutai one of the world's fifty most innovative for the second straight year. The company currently employs around 20 000 workers and has an annual production capacity of 40 000 tonnes and rising.

LANGJIU 郎酒

Laolangjiu 1956
老郎酒 1956
Sauce Aroma
53% ABV
Ingredients: Sorghum

'Old Lang' has a pungent nose with hints of soy and fermenting grains. A very savoury baijiu with a long finish that is tangy verging on sour.

Good fortune has placed Langjiu Distillery at the dividing line between Chinese baijiu's two most celebrated categories. Erlang Distillery was built on the banks of the Chishui River along the Sichuan-Guizhou border, almost equidistant from Luzhou and Maotai, respective origins of strong and sauce aromas. But for most of its history, Langjiu's fate has been more closely tied to the latter.

Erlang and Maotai both became famous for their baijiu in the late nineteenth century, when they were distribution centres for the imperial salt monopoly. The trade brought them both wealth and, more importantly, the latest northern distillation techniques. In 1898 Erlang stopped producing small-qu baijiu *and* within decades it was producing spirits nearly indistinguishable from those in Maotai. When Maotai raised the price on its

Three-Star Guibin Lang
三星贵宾郎
Strong Aroma
50% ABV
Ingredients: Sorghum

Strawberry and cherry headline its notably fruity bouquet. An aggressively sharp pineapple flavour attacks the palate before a bitter finish.

baijiu, Erlang followed suit – a practice that has endured to the present. They even share Premier Zhou Enlai, patron saint of Kweichow Moutai, who in 1956 suggested the government revitalise Erlang's baijiu industry. The next year the state-run Langjiu Distillery opened its doors for business.

Langjiu is currently the penultimate sauce-aroma producer by sales volume. It has an annual output of 30 000 tonnes of sauce aroma, but it no longer shuns the baijiu of its Sichuanese brethren. In the 1980s, when strong-aroma baijiu skyrocketed in popularity, Langjiu imitated its sister distillery in Luzhou and began producing strong- and mixed-aroma products. Since the 1970s, it has aged its best baijius in Erlang's two cliff-side 'treasure' caves, a onetime hideaway for the Taiping Army.

LIDU 郎酒

Lidu Town, Nanchang County, Jiangxi | www.lidujiu.com

Lidujiu 6 Year
李渡酒六年陈
Strong Aroma
52% ABV
Ingredients: Rice, wheat, sorghum

Lidujiu incorporates a three-grain mash with the type of wheat-bran and pea qu normally associated with northern baijiu. A rich and aromatic offering with notes of soy and dried herbs.

The village of Lidu, located in a remote region of a province not typically known for baijiu, is an unintuitive location for China's earliest spirits. But in 2012 archaeologists unearthed there an 800-year-old distillery, the most ancient ever discovered. These findings may not prove that Jiangxi was baijiu's birthplace, but they have lent credence to the historical records that pinpoint the Yuan Dynasty (1271–1368) as a moment when Chinese first distilled spirits. Lidu distillers passed down their craft to successive generations, culminating in the formation of the state-run Lidu Distillery in 1956 from the amalgamation of the town's nine most famous private distilleries. With an annual production capacity of more than 15 000 tonnes, it is a leading producer of strong-aroma baijiu in southeastern China and became part of the VATS Group in 2008.

Liuyanghe 50 Year
浏 阳 河 50 年
Strong Aroma
52% ABV
Ingredients: Sorghum, rice, glutinous rice, wheat, corn

A hint of fermented tofu and chamomile on the nose, and an aggressively alcoholic body with lots of citrus fruit. Tingles in the throat long after departing.

BAIJIUS

Although historic records indicate that Liuyang has been producing alcohol for more than a thousand years, Hunan has only recently become noteworthy for its baijiu. Liuyang established its first well-known distillery, Meilichang, at the start of the twentieth century. By mid-century, the Communist Party under Hunan-native Mao Zedong assumed control of the government and with it the baijiu industry. The government merged Meilichang and a handful of other baijiu workshops in 1956 to form the Liuyanghe Distillery, whose flagship product was appropriately named 'Red Classic'. In 1998, the Hunan Zhongshan Group purchased Liuyanghe and coordinated with strong-aroma titan Wuliangye to redevelop the brand. Publicly listed since 2011, Liuyanghe produces one of central China's leading strong aromas and has an annual production capacity of 36 000 tonnes.

BAIJIU: THE ESSENTIAL GUIDE TO CHINESE SPIRITS

Guose Jingdian
国色经典
Strong Aroma
50% ABV
Ingredients: Sorghum

An aggressive strong aroma with a creamy nose and flavours of roasted herbs and red berry jam. Has a hot and biting finish.

In Chinese lore, Luoyang-native Du Kang is the Prometheus of Chinese alcohol. An imperial minister (and later emperor) who allowed grain stores to go off, Du Kang smelled the sickly sweet fragrance of rotting grain and found his calling. He is credited with inventing sorghum alcohol, and later legends suggest that his wine could induce three years of perpetual drunkenness. As the ancient warlord Cao Cao once famously wrote, 'I know but one wine: Du Kang.'

Luoyang used to have two duelling Du Kang baijius, located in neighbouring Yichuan and Ruyang counties. In 2009, after almost four decades of hard fought war, the Du Kangs declared an armistice and formed the Luoyang Dukang Distillery. It is one of the leading strong-aroma producers in northern China.

National Cellar 1573
国窖1573
Strong Aroma
52% ABV
Ingredients: Sorghum

The cream of Luzhou Laojiao, 1573 has a fruity, floral taste with touches of liquorice and a hot peppery finish. It is a well-balanced and smooth baijiu.

Located at the confluence of the Tuo and Yangtze Rivers in southeastern Sichuan, Luzhou Laojiao has the longest continuous history of any Chinese distillery. Luzhou has been a regional winemaking hub for more than 2 000 years, but is believed to have begun distilling spirits during or shortly after the Song Dynasty (960–1279). During the subsequent Yuan Dynasty, Guo Huaiyu became the first Luzhou distiller to work with big qu in 1324. In 1425, Shi Jingzhang developed the city's world-famous pit fermentation method, consequently inventing strong-aroma baijiu. Shu Chengzong inherited Shi's technique in the sixteenth century and built fermentation pits still in use by the Luzhou Laojiao ('Old Pit') Distillery.

When the Chinese government relocated its capital to nearby Chongqing during the Second World War, Luzhou baijiu »

BAIJIUS

Tequ Laojiu
特曲老酒
Strong Aroma
52% ABV
Ingredients: Sorghum

A baijiu that explodes on the palate; tastes of apple rounded out by an alcoholic singe and a marshmallow finish.

developed rapidly and reached an annual production level of 1800 tonnes. In 1951, the government merged dozens of the city's principal liquor producers into the Luzhou Laojiao Distillery. Eight years later, Luzhou Laojiao literally wrote the book on strong-aroma baijiu: *Luzhou Laojiao Big Qu Liquor*, which the government prepared to instruct other fledging state-owned distilleries in making exceptional spirits. Before the book's publication, all baijiu production techniques were passed down orally, and now there was a textbook.

At the heart of Luzhou-style baijiu is the 'thousand-year fermentation pit, ten-thousand-year mash' technique, which repeatedly ferments and distils the same mash in an unending cycle. Fresh grains are added in each time and the mash is always returned to the same mud fermentation pit. Over time

Ming River
明江
Strong Aroma
45% ABV
Ingredients: Sorghum

Currently available exclusively outside of China, Ming River Sichuan Baijiu is a drink intended for both the bar and the restaurant. On the palate is a burst of pineapple tempered with anise and a smooth, creamy texture.

the pit develops a thick patina of bacteria and fungus that aids in fermentation and improves the character of the alcohol.

Strong-aroma baijiu distillers believe the older the pit, the better the baijiu, and for a pit to be considered 'old', it needs to have been in continuous use for at least thirty years. On that count, no one can approach Luzhou Laojiao, which has 1619 old pits. Of these pits, more than a thousand are at least a century old and the oldest dates from 1573. National Cellar 1573, Luzhou Laojiao's top shelf label, is produced using mash fermented in that pit and aged in caves for at least five years.

Under Chairman Mao, Luzhou Laojiao's standard big-qu baijiu was a staple on Sichuanese dinner tables, but the distillery struggled to keep pace with the rapid development of the baijiu industry and fell behind some of its less storied Sichuanese »

Touqu
头曲
Strong Aroma
52% ABV
Ingredients: Sorghum, rice, wheat

Touqu or 'Top Qu' is a sweeter, gentler baijiu intended for casual drinking. It offers exceptional value for the mid-range bracket.

competitors in the 1980s. The release of National Cellar 1573 in 2001, however, succeeded in bringing Luzhou Laojiao back into the national spotlight.

Today Luzhou Laojiao has reclaimed a position as one of the nation's most valuable brands, behind only Moutai, Wuliangye and Yanghe. It remains the unquestioned leader in simple-grain strong-aroma baijiu, but also produces a diverse range of spirits available domestically and abroad. It is also one of the nation's biggest producers by volume, with a stated annual production capacity of over 100 000 tonnes and plans for further expansion.

In 2018 Luzhao Laojiao formed Ming River with four baijiu enthusiasts (including the author), becoming the first major distillery to create a baijiu for non-Chinese consumers.

Niulanshan Erguotou

牛 栏 山 二 锅 头

Light Aroma

56% ABV

Ingredients: Sorghum

Currently one of the top-two erguotou brands, this is a gentle and easy to drink baijiu with an almost imperceptible touch of apricot in the finish.

During the Qing Dynasty – the high-water mark of Beijing erguotou – the spirits of Niulanshan stood a class apart. Northeast of the walled city on the banks of the Chaobai River, Niulanshan Town was blessed with a temperate climate, abundant produce and, most important, close proximity to Beijing's dissolute scholar-officials. Records from the waning days of the empire indicate that Niulanshan had hundreds of workers employed by a dozen major distilleries, all jockeying for use of the sublime well water in front of Golden Bull Cave. Over time Niulanshan's name became synonymous with high-quality erguotou. The trains of baijiu-bearing mule carts embarking from Niulanshan supposedly extended to the gates of the old city walls, and Niulanshan spirits could be purchased as far away as Tianjin. »

BAIJIUS

NIULANSHAN 牛栏山

Chenniang
陈酿
Strong-aroma Style
42% ABV
Ingredients: Sorghum

An inexpensive but popular faux baijiu, it uses neutral baijiu flavoured to taste like strong-aroma. Strong tropical fruit with a dry, herby notes.

In 1952, Gonglihao, Fushucheng and several other leading private distilleries were merged into the Niulanshan Distillery. In its early years of operation the factory's scale of operations was small, no more than fifty employees, but the company's rise to national prominence has been rapid since the 1970s. Today Niulanshan claims the largest production capacity of any independent Chinese distillery – 150 000 tonnes – recently closing the gap with its chief erguotou competitor, Red Star, in terms of sales and popularity. The company attributes this success to the preservation of its unique culture and heritage, maintaining production in its original factory and keeping diligent records of the experiences of past employees and specialists for posterity.

Ganbei
干杯
Strong Aroma
52% ABV
Ingredients: Sorghum, rice, glutinous rice, wheat, corn

Subject to little tweaking, this is one of the most authentic 'American' baijius. Sorghum and the two rice strains give it a nose of aniseed and butterscotch with an assertive and fruity alcoholic bite.

BAJIUS

Chicago-native Richard Przekop is one of those rare foreign drinkers who loved baijiu upon first sip. Charged with opening a new company office in Shanghai, he instead became enamoured of Chinese spirits and decided to bring his passion back with him to the United States. Soon after leaving China, he established Project Spirits with Beijing-born partner Jessica Ji.

Project Spirits' Ganbei, named after the battle cry of the raucous Chinese drinker, is produced start-to-finish in Sichuan with an original recipe tailored to the Western market. Project Spirits believes that the greatest obstacle to the acceptance of baijiu overseas is education, and to that end is, at the outset, exclusively targeting bars and restaurants.

RED STAR 红星

Beijing | www.redstarwine.com

Hongxing Erguotou
红星二锅头
Light Aroma
56% ABV
Ingredients: Sorghum

This basic, somewhat phenolic baijiu is what most people have in mind when they say 'erguotou'. As a bonus, its cap can be (and often is) used as a shot glass in a pinch.

Red Star, or Hongxing, is the Coca-cola of Chinese spirits. Available for a fistful of change at any convenience store in China, its economy, simplicity and consistent quality have made it a staple of the Chinese working class diet the nation over. If Moutai is the drink of the Chinese elite, Hongxing Erguotou is the drink of the Chinese everyman.

The company traces its origins back to the Zhao brothers, whose Yuanshenghao Distillery invented the erguotou style in 1680. Beijing distillers at the time called the still's condenser (the part that cools alcoholic vapour into liquid) the *tianguo* or 'heavenly pot'. Because the temperature of the water used as coolant in the *tianguo* would rapidly rise, it needed to be replaced twice during distillation. The Zhaos discovered that the alcohol produced during the second of three pots – the

Redstar
红 星
Light Aroma
43% ABV
Ingredients: Sorghum

This sleek, modern hip-flask-style
bottle is well worth the slight
price upgrade. A light and mild
baijiu with notes of sweet pomelo
in the nose and a long finish.

heart of the spirit – was the finest, and begun selling it as the
erguotou or 'second pot head'.

From the name Red Star, one might rightly infer the distillery's
Communist origins. Red Star received the first business licence
issued by the People's Republic of China, when it was hastily
thrown together in April 1949 to produce alcohol for the
nation's inaugural ceremony on 1 October of the same year. The
government brought together twelve of Beijing's most respected
private distilleries to form one state-run erguotou giant in the
northern city's Huairou District. A Japanese Red Army enlistee
named Sakurai designed the brand's distinctive label.

Red Star remains one of China's best-selling baijiu brands by
volume and has the fastest production speed of any baijiu distillery, capable of bottling an astonishing 30 000 units an hour.

SANSU 三苏

Taihe Town, Meishan, Sichuan | www.sansujiu.com.cn

Su Dongpo
苏 东 坡
Strong Aroma
52% ABV
Ingredients: Sorghum,
glutinous rice, wheat

Named for the most famous
of the Three Sus, and the most
enthusiastic drinker of the trio,
Su Dongpo is Sansu's upmarket
baijiu. A fiery and unyielding spirit.

Meishan sits at the base of the mountains south of Chengdu along the banks of the Min River. In the twelfth century, it was home to Su Xun and his sons Su Dongpo and Su Zhe. The Three Sus (*San Su*), as they are affectionately known, were likely China's most talented literary family, comprising a dominant bloc of the Eight Masters of Tang and Song Prose.

The local government formed the Taihe Distillery in 1956 by merging two late-imperial distilleries that specialised in small-qu baijiu, like those still popular in Chongqing. A year later, the factory switched to big-qu strong-aroma baijiu. The distillery changed its name to Sansu in 1984, and went private in 2000. A medium-sized distillery, it currently produces 10 000 tonnes annually.

Yubingshao
玉 冰 烧
Chi Aroma
29% ABV
Ingredients: Rice

Yubingshao is a light and somewhat oily baijiu. Has the sweet taste of longan fruit and a bit of bacon on the back end.

BAIJIUS

The Cantonese have long been chided with the now cliché remark that they will 'eat anything on four legs except the table', but a better-kept secret is the fact that they will also drink it. In 1984, Shiwan Distillery distinguished itself from other local rice baijiu producers when it decided to round out its flavour with the addition of pork in the aging process. It called this Semitic nightmare of a spirit Yubingshao ('Jade Ice Spirit'), and its category, chi aroma, after a condiment made of salty fermented beans popular in southern China.

The technique of infusing wine and spirits with pork, used almost exclusively in Guangdong Province, requires careful scrutiny. If the baijiu oxidises too much, it can develop an unpleasant greasy aspect. At least least one or two years' time is required for the liquid to fully absorb the swine's flavour. »

Yubingshao 6 Year
玉 冰 烧 六 年
Chi Aroma
33% ABV
Ingredients: Rice, glutinous rice

A bit more sharply chemical and a lot less sweetness than the standard variety, this spirit has a pleasant, mild burn in the finish.

This process resembles the ancient north Chinese practice of infusing wines with lamb, fuelling speculation that it was brought south by immigrants from the Central Chinese Plains – perhaps the rice-wine loving Hakkas. A man named Chen, who spurned an official imperial career to take over the family distillery, first introduced pork infusions to Foshan in 1895. Shiwan Distillery, the ancestor of the Chen clan's shop, has existed in its current incarnation since 1951.

Yuanjiang
原浆
Strong Aroma
52% ABV
Ingredients: Sorghum , rice, glutinous rice, corn, wheat

Rich in aroma and balanced in flavour, this is a delicate, sweet liquor that offers good value for its category. The ceramic lid doubles as a baijiu glass.

BAIJIUS

Not to be confused with Shaanxi-based Taibai, Shixian Taibai takes its name from the style name of the *shixian* ('immortal poet'), Li Bai, who passed through Wanzhou on one of many drunken jaunts. The distillery's history is long but borrowed. In 1917, Chongqing businessman Bao Nianrong purchased mud from two Ming Dynasty fermentation pits owned by Wen Yongsheng Distillery in Luzhou (ancestor to modern-day Luzhou Laojiao). Transporting the precious, bacteria-rich mud downstream to the Three Gorges, Bao established the Hualinchun Distillery at Wanzhou, which would later become Shixian Taibai. The company recently invested RMB171 million (US$28 million) to build a vast new distillery in Qionglai, which will bring its annual production capacity to above 60000 tonnes.

BAIJIU: THE ESSENTIAL GUIDE TO CHINESE SPIRITS

Zhenbaofang Junfang
珍宝坊君坊
Strong Aroma
41.8% and 68% ABV
Ingredients: Sorghum

A split-level baijiu with 68% *yuanjiu* in the bottle cap. Has an attractive aroma with notes of strawberry and lychee. Smooth and gentle with a rambling finish.

Jiangsu natives neatly sum up their advice to visitors in rhyming couplets: 'See the sights of Yangzhou, drink the drinks of Shuanggou'. Shuanggou Town's winemaking tradition extends back more than fifteen centuries, but consisted mainly of huangjiu. In 1732 a Shanxi distiller surnamed He sojourned to the south and, attracted by the Huai River and the local sorghum, decided to settle in Shuanggou. He substituted big qu for the then popular small qu, and the region's distillers followed suit. By the early twentieth century, Shuanggou had more than forty big-qu distilleries. Soon after Jiangsu fell to the Japanese in 1938, the local baijiu industry collapsed, but the town's Communist sympathies prior to occupation helped spur its rehabilitation after the war. Yanghe, Shuanggou's chief regional rival, purchased a controlling stake in the distillery in 2008.

Shuhuaiqianxing
抒怀遣兴
Sauce Aroma
53% ABV
Ingredients: Sorghum

An aromatic baijiu with a strong aroma of dark soy and caramelised fruit. Has a long and lingering aftertaste.

BAJIUS

Maotai is a remote village, sealed off by treacherous mountain passes, but it has as high a concentration of distilleries as can be found almost anywhere on the planet. The success of hometown hero Kweichow Moutai has created a local economy in which every family has a stake in the baijiu trade, and countless distilleries, sauce aroma or otherwise, have sprung up in the region. Shuhuaiqianxing is one of the many producers riding on the coat-tails of its progenitor. Though none has the name recognition of Moutai, many local distilleries have started producing comparable products at far more affordable prices. Others have tried to diversify their product ranges with new categories. Shuhuaiqianxing does both, having produced solid sauce-aroma and sesame-aroma products since 1997.

SHUI JING FANG 水井坊

Wellbay
经台装
Strong Aroma
52% ABV
Ingredients: Sorghum, rice, glutinous rice, wheat, corn

It might sound like a fitness drink, but Shui Jing Fang's signature blend refers to the well from which the ancient distillery sprung. It is an intense but smooth spirit, with a fruity aroma and a touch of anise.

Shui Jing Fang hearkens back to the glory days of Chengdu wine-making. According to historical record, Sichuan was home to more than a thousand distilleries by the mid-nineteenth century, but little trace of this legacy has survived in the provincial capital. So it was with great interest that the ruins of a 600-year-old distillery were discovered during routine factory renovations at the Quanxing Distillery on Chengdu's Shui Jing ('Water Well') Street in 1998. With furnaces, cooling grounds and fermentation pits at various depths, the site revealed the distillation history of successive eras literally stacked on top of one another. It was the oldest distillery unearthed in southwest China.

Any good baijiu brand requires a compelling backstory, and Quanxing had inadvertently stumbled upon a great one. In 2000, the Chengdu distillery released its first high-end baijiu,

Forest Green
菁 翠
Strong Aroma
52% ABV

Ingredients: Sorghum rice, glutinous rice, wheat, corn

A step up from Wellbay, Forest Green is filtered with charcoal and bamboo, which mellows out some of the more pungent aromas and gives it a crisp, even finish.

Shui Jing Fang, whose mud-lined fermentation pits contained yeast cultures harvested from the ruins. Three years later, British spirits giant Diageo entered into a joint venture with Quanxing, which established Shui Jing Fang as an independent brand. This partnership was founded on the basis of combining Quanxing's brewing prowess with Diageo's global distribution network and knowhow to create the first truly international baijiu. The result was a sophisticated baijiu that incorporates several production techniques new to the Chinese alcohol world.

In the span of a decade, Shui Jing Fang has become a ubiquitous top-shelf baijiu, widely available throughout the country and often mentioned in the same breath as Moutai or Wuliangye. At the cost of hundreds of millions of pounds, Diageo has continually increased its share of the company »

Tianhaochen
天号陈
Strong Aroma
45% ABV
Ingredients: Sorghum, rice, glutinous rice, wheat, corn

A good quality mid-range product intended for mass-market consumption, Tianhaochen has many of the same flavours as its sister baijius but with slightly less refinement.

and now holds a controlling stake. Though Shui Jing Fang's swift ascension has been impressive, whether its steep investment will pay off will depend largely on the company's ability to establish a foothold overseas. Shui Jing Fang is already popular with Korean consumers, who are accustomed to drinking soju, a near relative of baijiu, and Diageo has begun pushing the brand into the European and North American markets.

Dongfangyun
东 方 韵
Special Aroma
42% ABV
Ingredients: Rice

It might smell a bit like pencil rubber, but on the tongue it has a beautiful balance of sweet and astringent flavours similar to tropical fruit.

BAIJIUS

In the nineteenth century, tavern keep Lou Xiulong invented Sitir's singular red-stone-brick pit fermentation style, which produces a spirit different in almost every respect from other rice baijius. The local practice at the time was to write the Chinese character for 'special' on the bamboo baskets that encased wine bottles, but Lou's spirit was so unique that it was given the singular honour of four 'special' characters – thus the name *Si Te* or 'four specials' (the modern distillery has opted for the inexplicable Sitir transliteration). In 1952, the government established Zhangshu (later Sitir) Distillery, employing various washed-up local distillers to create a new spirit based on Lou's methods. Sitir gained national acclaim on the praise of such luminaries as Zhou Enlai, who noted its 'pure light aroma and rich aftertaste'. It is now the sole representative of special-aroma baijiu.

Xijing
西京
Phoenix Aroma
45% ABV
Ingredients: Sorghum, wheat, rice

Xijing or 'Western Capital' evokes fermented soy mixed with a mild floral sweetness in the nose. Chrysanthemum is the predominant taste, but a pungency develops in the smooth finish.

In the heyday of Xifengjiu's phoenix-aroma baijiu, distilleries across northern China produced Shaanxi's signature style. But phoenix aroma's harshness, combined with the relative popularity of strong aroma have increasingly made it a regional category better suited to the fiery cuisine and rough temperament of the northwest. Even the provincial capital's Xi'an Distillery has taken to producing strong aroma. But Taibai Distillery persists and excels in the waning local tradition.

The producer gets its name from Baoji's Taibai Mountain, which in turn is named for China's drunken immortal, the master poet Li Bai. China likes its poets and loves its drinkers, and few men so ably wore both hats as Li Bai. During the eighth century, Li served at the court of the Tang Dynasty at what is now Xi'an. As his friend and contemporary Du Fu

Taibaizui
太白醉
Phoenix Aroma
45% ABV
Ingredients: Sorghum, wheat, rice

With a clay bottle in the shape of a 'Drunken Li Bai', this baijiu's fragrance resembles candied banana, but the taste is earthier than Xijing. Has a long, tingly finish.

relates, alcohol fuelled Li's creative genius and the taverns of Xi'an became his second home – or at least where he wound up sleeping most nights.

Given its proximity to the Tang court Mei County's winemakers began flourishing around the time that Li Bai graced the earth. Using water from Taibai Mountain's Bingdou Lake, Mei distillers later began producing sorghum spirits in the style of nearby Fengxiang County by the late imperial era. By 1949, the county had almost fifty independent distillers, six of which were combined to create Taibai Distillery in 1956. By the 1980s, its spirits started achieving national recognition and in 2009, it was acquired by Beijing spirits conglomerate VATS Group. Its current annual production capacity is 20 000 tonnes.

TAIWAN TOBACCO & LIQUOR
台灣煙酒

Taipei, Taiwan | liquor.ttl.com.tw

Yushan Kaoliang
3 Year
于山高粱 3 年
Light Aroma
58% ABV
Ingredients: Sorghum

Yushan has a distinctly floral aroma with hints of chrysanthemum and osmanthus. It has a lingering finish that is quite smooth despite the strength.

At the instigation of Chiang Ching-kuo (son of Generalissimo Chiang Kai-shek), the alcohol division of state-run Taiwan Tobacco and Liquor Corporation established its first and only baijiu distillery in 1950. The initial production site was Chiayi Distillery, a former Japanese wine and spirits producer in southern Taiwan. The new baijiu, Taiwan's first after the revolution, was called Yushan or 'Jade Mountain' after the island's highest peak. Yushan later expanded its production base to include the Longtian Distillery in neighbouring Tainan. Yushan is considered a *gaoliang*, the Taiwanese answer to Beijing erguotou, usually bottled at 38% or 58% ABV. All of Yushan Kaoliang's spirits are distilled three times and aged at least six months.

Taizi

太紫

Light Aroma
58% ABV
Ingredients: Sorghum

This is as close as baijiu gets to vodka, particularly in the nose. It has a smooth body with notes of violet and apricot and a long peppery finish, which hangs in the mouth and warms the belly.

BAIJIUS

Papa Lu brought the family from Taiwan to New Zealand in the 1990s, and with them a recipe. A cargo ship captain by trade, he spent his off hours brewing the Taiwan-style *gaoliang* he had learned while serving at Kinmen. After their father passed away, Ben and Sam Lu dusted their stills and conceived a baijiu that could be both a stepping stone for the Western world and a New World baijiu for the Chinese. The brothers Lu teamed up with Southern Grain Spirits' master distiller John Fitzpatrick, who tweaked the baijiu's production, most notably in distillation: using a rare English copper column still manufactured by John Dore in 1835. In 2009, the Lu brothers founded New Zealand Chinese Liquor, which released its first spirit in 2013. Taizi is made with ingredients sourced from New Zealand and Australia, and is filtered not aged.

TIANLONG HUANGHELOU
天 龙 黄 鹤 楼

Wuhan, Hubei | www.hhljy.com.cn

Huanghelou 8 Year
黄 鹤 楼 8 年
Mixed Aroma
42% ABV
Ingredients: Sorghum, wheat, glutinous rice, rice, corn

An understated crowd-pleaser with sour apple in the nose and a mild pineapple taste. A smooth and refreshing liquor with a brief finish.

Tianlong Huanghelou tests the efficacy of the current baijiu classification system: Its flagship Tezhi or 'Specially Produced' baijiu is listed as mixed aroma, but blends aspects of light and strong rather than strong and sauce. This distinction is rooted in Wuhan's distilling tradition. In 1662, Wuhan first produced spirits using medicinal wheat qu. By the late nineteenth century, the provincial capital had over a hundred distilleries, the most famous of which distilled pit-fermented spirits and a light aroma called Han Fenjiu, after Shanxi's Fenjiu style. The Han Fenjiu distilleries served as the foundation of the Wuhan Distillery, which opened in 1952 and released its first mixed-aroma baijiu a decade later. The distillery changed its name to Huanghelou, for Wuhan's famous Yellow Crane Pagoda, and currently produces more than 10 000 tonnes of baijiu annually.

Tujiaren
土 家 人
Strong Aroma
52% ABV
Ingredients: Sorghum, rice, wheat, glutinous rice, corn

Tujiaren has a layered flavour profile that includes hints of rice, herbs and nuts, and a spicy, somewhat bitter finish.

Tujiaren is named for the Tujia people, one of China's fifty-five officially recognised minority groups, most of whom live along the border of Hunan, Hubei and Guizhou Provinces. The Tujia trace their origins to the ancient Ba Kingdom in what is now Chongqing, and it is this Sichuanese tradition that inspires Tujiaren baijiu. A private distillery established in the Xiangxi Tujia and Miao Autonomous Region in 2000, Tujiaren produces mixed-grain strong-aroma baijiu using several fermentation-distillation cycles. As a brand, it is best known for its exclusive use of traditional style ceramic bottles. It is a small distillery that produces only a few thousand tonnes of baijiu annually.

Shede
舍 得
Strong Aroma
52% ABV
Ingredients: Sorghum, rice, glutinous rice, wheat, corn, barley

The distillery's premium brand, Shede is an exceptionally sweet and mild strong aroma, smelling of moist grains and exuding an almost chocolaty taste with notes of roasted barley.

While making a pilgrimage to the hometown of Tang poet Chen Zi'ang, the eighth century master-poet Du Fu composed a verse celebrating the 'cool, green wine of Shehong'. As Chen and Du Fu's fame grew, so too did that of Shehong's wine, and by the Song Dynasty writers already considered it to be among the empire's most revered libations. By the late imperial period, Shehong's Tai An Distillery began distilling a spirit from glutinous rice, sorghum and wheat known as Xiejiu, forming a foundation for one of the so-called Six Golden Flowers of Sichuan, Tuopai baijiu.

The name Tuopai or 'Tuo Brand' derives from Shehong's Tuo Spring, which has formed the base of the town's wines since the time of Du Fu. The Tuopai Daqu Distillery was established by the government in 1951, and was later renamed Tuopai Shede after the company's most popular premium baijiu.

Tuopai Touqu
沱牌头曲
Strong Aroma
50% ABV
Ingredients: Sorghum, rice, glutinous rice, wheat, corn, barley

One seldom describes a baijiu as refreshing, but Tuopai fits the bill. A smooth spirit that tastes of rainwater and cucumber with floral overtones. Sweetens to lemon in the finish.

The distillery's signature blend is a six-grain mash, adding barley to the standard mixed-grain recipe. Its baijius are famous for their grainy aromas and sweet body, said to derive from the use of Manchurian rice. Tuopai Shede became a publicly-listed company in 1996, and currently controls more than twenty subsidiary companies, mostly related to alcohol production. It is one of the largest producers in Sichuan, with more than 7 000 employees and an annual production capacity of more than 30 000 tonnes.

Vinn Baijiu
Rice Aroma
40% ABV
Ingredients: Brown rice

Currently the only baijiu made entirely in the United States, Vinn has touches of sticky rice and lemon curd in its nose and a floral, somewhat nutty flavour. A highly delicate spirit.

Vinn's proprietors, the Ly family, originally hail from Vietnam's Quang Ninh Province, just across the border from China's Guangxi Province. In the lead-up to the 1979 Sino-Vietnamese War, the Vietnamese government deported the Ly's ethnically Chinese village. After arriving in China, the Lys made a harrowing fifty-seven-day journey on a fishing boat to seek asylum in Hong Kong and ultimately settled in Oregon. Patriarch Phan Ly brought the seven-generation-old family baijiu recipe to the United States. When Phan retired from the restaurant business, his children started Vinn Distillery so that he could focus on his passion. Though he wanted to call the business Five Siblings, the five siblings overruled him and picked Vinn, their common middle name. Vinn produces *mijiu*, baijiu and vodka, currently available in the Pacific Northwest.

文君 WENJUN

www.wenjun.com.cn | Qionglai, Sichuan

Wenjunjiu
文君酒
Strong Aroma
52% ABV
Ingredients: Sorghum, rice, glutinous rice, wheat, corn

Wenjunjiu is a smooth baijiu with aniseed in the nose and soft notes of banana and toasted rice on the palate. The sleek bottle is intended to resemble a traditional Chinese lute.

Wenjun traces its origins back to the early Han Dynasty (206BC–220AD), when Zhuo Wenjun, the beautiful daughter of a Sichuanese official, eloped from Chengdu to Qionglai with scholar-official Sima Xiangru. Without her family's blessing, the couple was forced into dignified poverty, selling their possessions and starting a wine shop. Wenjun excelled in winemaking and Qionglai became a regional alcohol hub.

The Wenjun Distillery, started in 1951, fell on hard times by the close of the twentieth century and was sold to Jiannanchun, who in turn sold a majority stake to Louis Vuitton Moët Hennessey in 2007 for US$141 million. Thereupon Wenjun suspended operations and relaunched its baijiu the next year with a new recipe by master blender Madame Wu Xiaoping, new packaging, and celebrity spokesperson: actor-director Jiang Wen.

BAIJIUS

Wuliangye
五 粮 液
Strong Aroma
52% ABV
Ingredients: Sorghum, rice, glutinous rice, wheat, corn

One of the best-selling high-end spirits in the world. Wuliangye's signature blend has a peppery nose and a complex yet balanced taste with strong notes of pineapple, liquorice and meadow grass.

Yibin lies in southeastern Sichuan, where the Min River meets the Jinsha River to form the Yangtze. It has a diverse culture and a long tradition of winemaking, dating back more than a thousand years. Yibin's alcohol industry began distilling baijiu at least as early as the Ming Dynasty (1368–1644) and still has sixteen operational fermentation pits from that era, placing it in the same era as provincial rival Luzhou Laojiao. In 2005, some of Wuliangye's Ming pit mud was harvested and donated to the National Museum of China.

But what put Yibin on the baijiu map was its recipe. During the Song Dynasty (960–1279) the Yao family of Yibin first developed a wine recipe that incorporated a complex blend of grains. The recipe passed from one family to another through the generations until 1900, when Chen San, the tenth in the

Wuliangchun
五 粮 春
Strong Aroma
50% ABV
Ingredients: Sorghum, rice, glutinous rice, wheat, corn

Wuliangye's mid-range sister brand, also available at 35% and 45% ABV, is somewhat fruitier and delivers a shorter, dry finish.

line of Chen clan distillers, concocted the five-grain recipe still used in today's Wuliangye, which had a spicy-sweet body with a bitter edge.

The only thing it lacked was the right handle. Since ancient times, the mixed-grain wines of Yibin were known as Yao Snow Qu to the literati and *zaliang jiu* or 'mixed-grain wine' to commoners. Local scholar Yang Huiquan tasted Yibin's mixed-grain wines in 1909 and declared the common name too vulgar and the more elegant name too obtuse. 'It would be more fitting', he suggested, 'that it be called Five Grain Liquid', or *Wuliangye*. The name stuck and the drink flourished.

In 1951 eight of Yibin's best traditional distilleries were consolidated into a single state-run distillery, the Yibin Distillery (Yibin Wuliangye Distillery after 1959). Distilled from a blend »

Wuliangchun
五粮醇
Strong Aroma
45% ABV
Ingredients: Sorghum, rice, glutinous rice, wheat, corn

A case study in linguistic confusion, Wuliangye's two Chun baijius are distinguished by mere tonal inflection. Chun (醇) is the lower-end of the pair, with a yeasty barnyard smell and a grassy body.

of sorghum, rice, glutinous rice, wheat and corn, its baijiu quickly became the standard-bearer of mixed-grain strong-aroma baijiu. On the strength of its premium spirits, Wuliangye had grown to become China's biggest distillery by sales volume by the 1990s. Wuliangye became a publicly listed company in 1998 and has interests in several spin-off distilleries, such as Jinliufu and Liuyanghe. In 2011, Wuliangye became the first Chinese brand to advertise in New York's Times Square. A year later, Yibin's government began construction on the Yibin Wuliangye Airport, whose name sparked minor controversy.

Today Wuliangye's massive production base covers 10 square kilometres, employs more than 40000 workers and has a stated annual output of 400000 tonnes.

Piaoxiang
飘香
Sauce Aroma
53% ABV
Ingredients: Sorghum

Piaoxiang or 'Floating Fragrance' smells of dark soy sauce and pencil rubber. Has a sharp alcoholic attack somewhat overpowered by a tinny flavour that turns to grape in a medium finish.

BAIJIUS

In antiquity, Changde was called Wuling and its most famous winemaker was the Cui family, or as recorded in verse, 'The city of Wuling has Cui Clan Wine; the earth has nothing so heavenly.' But the story of contemporary Wuling begins with its predecessor, Changde Distillery, in 1952. Whenever Mao visited his home province of Hunan, stops along his itinerary were instantly elevated into patriotic pilgrimage sites. Unfortunately for visiting officials, Hunan's annual Kweichow Moutai ration was a half tonne or about a thousand bottles. Fortunately for Changde Distillery, factory manager Bao Peisheng's old classmate, Ji Keliang, was the technical vice director (and later chairman) of Kweichow Moutai. Together they developed Hunan's first sauce aroma, unveiled in 1972. Today Wuling also produces strong- and mixed-aroma baijius.

Fengxiang Jingdian
凤香经典
Phoenix Aroma
52% ABV
Ingredients: Sorghum

This 'Classic Phoenix Aroma' has a fresh nose with touches of cherry and pine, and a scorching hot body. Finishes with a syrupy sweetness.

Xifengjiu is the northwestern baijiu. As the originator and standard-bearer of *feng xiang* or phoenix aroma, it is one of the two most revered northern Chinese spirits (along with Xinghuacun Fenjiu). Xifengjiu was established in 1956 as a state-run distillery, but the style of winemaking from which it sprung has a history of more than 4000 years.

Long before Qin Shihuang first unified the nation in 221BC and established his court at Xianyang (modern day Xi'an), nearby Fengxiang was making wines of great depth and variety. According to legend, Fengxiang was where the 'phoenixes took flight' (*feng xiang*) – the root of the name Xifengjiu or 'Western Phoenix Spirit'. While posted as magistrate there in the eleventh century, the writer Su Dongpo wrote one of his most famous lines, 'When the flowers are in bloom and the wine is

Xifengjiu
西凤酒
Phoenix Aroma
55% ABV
Ingredients: Sorghum

The original, most basic phoenix aroma has a tart smell of green apples and wet grass, and an earthy taste that expands in the finish.

sweet, one can drink without drunkenness.' And while he was almost certainly writing about one of the traditional huangjius, the drinks shared many commonalities with the later baijius. By the early seventeenth century Fengxiang and its neighbouring villages were already producing Xifeng spirits at almost fifty distilleries.

Northwestern Chinese consider Shaanxi's biting spirits the perfect reflection of their famously gruff temperament but they also betray the region's ingenuity. Fengxiang distillers ferment their grains in mud pits similar to those used to create strong-aroma baijiu, but unlike their southern cousins they strip the mud away and apply a fresh coat each year. Phoenix aroma is also fermented in short, high-temperature cycles of about ten days each. The most defining feature of the category is its »

Xifeng 6 Year
西 凤 六 年 陈 酿
Phoenix Aroma
45% ABV
Ingredients: Sorghum

More complex than the un-aged iteration, it smells of dried fruit. The stunning finish is the real prize, with subtle notes of honey-dew in the aftertaste.

use of the 'seas of alcohol', aging receptacles that can hold as much as ten tonnes of raw distillate. They are constructed by applying hardened hemp paper to the inside of willow baskets. These vessels age the spirits more quickly than traditional ceramic urns and give Xifengjiu its distinctive flavour.

Xifengjiu possesses some of the best features of both light- and strong-aroma baijiu, leading some to suggest lumping it together with mixed-aroma baijiu, but it has little in common with other products in that category. A compromise was reached in 1992, when the Ministry of Light Industry established the phoenix-aroma category.

Today the Xifengjiu Distillery has an annual production capacity of close to 50 000 tonnes.

Laobai Fenchiew
老白汾酒
Light Aroma
53% ABV
Ingredients: Sorghum

The classic Laobai Fenjiu (written *fenchiew* in the antiquated Romanisation) has a mild floral nose and a strong taste of roasted rice and pine. Its porcelain lid doubles as a baijiu glass.

BAIJIUS

Xinghuacun Fenjiu is the single most important distillery in all of north China, the largest and heaviest drinking region of the county. Fenjiu has inspired almost every light-aroma baijiu of note, from the *gaoliang* of Taiwan to the Han Fenjiu of Hubei Province. Both in technique and choice of ingredients, the style is rooted in north-central China's Shanxi Province.

During the Ming Dynasty and Qing Dynasty, when Chinese spirits began to assume their modern form, the alcohol of the north had no rival. Despite being a southerner himself, even leading seventeenth century scholar Qian Qianyi wrote, 'I bitterly love the alcohol of the north; its rich fragrance spills into my dreams'. Most celebrated among them were the wines of Fenzhou (now Fenyang), from which the Fenjiu appellation derives. At first Fenjiu was a broad category that included grain »

Zishaci Fenjiu
紫砂瓷汾酒
Light Aroma
53% ABV
Ingredients: Sorghum

Bottled in China's prized purple clay (*zisha*) commonly used to make outstanding teapots. This is a richly layered baijiu with a savoury mixture of roasted herbs and pine.

wines, fruit wines and even an inexplicably popular lamb wine, but over time Fenzhou's spirits or 'fire wine' surpassed them all to become a nationally famous baijiu.

Two technological innovations define the Fenjiu style. The first is its use of barley and pea qus, several varieties of which are produced during the warmer summer months to promote microbial growth. The second is the process of burying and insulating its ceramic fermentation jars, which facilitates high-temperature fermentation throughout the frigid northern winters. The resulting alcohol is delicate, complex and extremely potent, characteristics all dear to the heart of Chinese alcohol aficionados.

In the Fenjiu school, the spirits brewed with Xinghuacun's sweet well water were considered the finest and regularly

Fenjiu
汾酒
Light Aroma
48% ABV
Ingredients: Sorghum

The most basic Fenjiu series. Has plums and floral notes in the nose, and a round, minty taste. Its pleasing finish is somewhat tart.

garnered awards at national exhibitions. By the early twentieth century, the village already had a number of famous distilleries and in 1919 private investors established there one of the nation's first modern distilleries, the Jinyu Fenjiu Corporation. Although at the time the province lacked the infrastructure to widely export Fenjiu, Jinyu was already producing about 40 tonnes a year by 1932. It was upon this firm foundation that the Xinghuacun Fenjiu Distillery was formed in the first year of the People's Republic.

Fenjiu also strikes the right patriotic chords so essential to the success of a Mainland baijiu. When Sun Yat-sen and Huang Xing met at a Tokyo Chinese restaurant in 1905, they toasted the destruction of the dissolute Manchu Qing Dynasty over glasses of Fenjiu. On the eve of his victory in the Chinese Civil »

Chu Yeh Ching Chiew
竹叶青酒
Light-Aroma Tonic
45% ABV
Ingredients: Sorghum, sweetener, bamboo leaves, gardenia, black cardamom

A popular medicinal baijiu. Has the bitter smell of TCM and nail polish remover that develops a rich sweetness reminiscent of ginger and brown sugar.

War, Mao Zedong smuggled Fenjiu into Henan via donkey cart for the enjoyment of visiting Soviet statesman Anastas Mikoyan. Mikoyan enjoyed Fenjiu so much that Mao served it to him again when he later visited a liberated Beijing. At the first session of the Chinese People's Political Consultative Conference in 1949, delegates toasted the birth of the New China with Laobai Fenjiu.

Xinghuacun Fenjiu is still considered the representative style of light-aroma baijiu and its distillery is one of the nation's largest baijiu producers. The distillery employs 10 000 workers (Xinghuacun's total population is 18 000) and has an annual production capacity of more than 75 000 tonnes.

洋 河 YANGHE

www.chinayanghe.com | Suqian, Jiangsu

Mengzhilan
梦 之 蓝
Strong Aroma
52% ABV
Ingredients: Sorghum, rice, glutinous rice, corn, wheat

A mixed-grain strong-aroma baijiu fermented with wheat-barley-pea-based qu, Mengzhilan ('Blue Dream') smells of honey and tastes of apricots and bean paste.

BAIJIUS

There's an old local saying about Yanghe spirits: 'When travellers smell it, they dismount their horses. When they've tasted it, they stop their carts.' And just a short distance to the Grand Canal, which facilitated water traffic to the Yellow River, Suqian used to get plenty of visitors. As Ming poet Zou Ji wrote, 'Many people pass through each year, but Yanghe liquor is what keeps them here.'

The modern Yanghe Distillery was established in 1949, but rose to national prominence in the late 1990s. It launched its premium Blue series baijiu in 2003, which bucked the established standard of red and gold packaging and catapulted the company forward to become one of the most valuable baijiu brands. In 2010, Yanghe bought out its chief regional competitor, Shuanggou, forming the Sujiu Corporation.

YINGCHUN 迎春

Langfang, Hebei | www.yingchunjiu.com

Yingchun
迎 春
Sauce Aroma
42% ABV
Ingredients: Sorghum

Smells like banana candy and liquorice, but the latter is the predominant flavour on the tongue. Finishes sweet but spicy. Surprising complexity for an entry-level baijiu.

Yingchun Distillery, sometimes called 'The North's Little Moutai', owes much of its reputation to the guidance of the late Zhou Henggang. A major figure in twentieth century baijiu, Zhou began his career as an engineer for his hometown distillery in Fushun, Liaoning. Following the revolution, he worked for the food division of the Ministry of Light Industry in Langfang, whose city distillery would later become Yingchun. Over the years Zhou became influential in just about every facet of baijiu production, leaving his biggest mark in the development and dissemination of bran-based qus, hallmark of northeastern sauce aroma. In 1984, Zhou assumed formal control of Yingchun's production and development. It is currently a mid-sized distillery, with an annual production capacity of 5000 tonnes.

Xiao Hutuxian
小糊涂仙
Strong Aroma
52% ABV
Ingredients: Sorghum

Xiao Hutuxian or 'Little Confused Immortal' has a layered aroma with creamy vanilla and nuts. The initial taste is savoury, but it finishes in a quick spicy burst underscored by pineapple.

BAIJIUS

Most newcomers struggle to gain a foothold in the crowded baijiu market, but not Yunfeng. The type of mega-corporation absent from countries with antitrust laws, the Guangzhou-based business has interests from electronics to hospitality. In 1997, Yunfeng deftly executed its plan: select the most popular category (strong aroma); build a factory in the nation's most famous booze town (Maotai); and guild its reputation by having the China Food Products Association host an expert tasting of its new Xiao Hutuxian baijiu. Its Chishui River factory opened in 2002 with a 10 000 tonne annual output and aging facilities in nearby caves. If the model for the twentieth century baijiu industry was state regulation and consolidation, Yunfeng heralds the capitalist, brand-driven future.

BAIJIU: THE ESSENTIAL GUIDE TO CHINESE SPIRITS

Hexie Qingya Renhe
和谐清雅人和
Mixed Aroma
42% ABV
Ingredients: Sorghum

With a name meaning 'harmonious elegance', the Hexie Qingya series is a well-balanced baijiu that smells of mild cheese and lemon curd with a pleasantly long and peppery finish.

The Yuquan Distillery hails from the ancient seat of the Jin Dynasty (1115–1234), just outside modern-day Harbin. Located in a famously scenic village surrounded by mountains, forests and the crystal clear streams from which it derives the name Yuquan or 'Jade Springs'. When the proto-Manchurian Jurchen people established their kingdom, Yuquan became the official wine supplier to the Jin court. Though it stretches the bounds of historical credibility, the distillery claims it was there that the Chinese invented *shaojiu* ('roasted wine' or spirits). Yuquan Town precipitously recedes from historical record after the Jin, briefly resurfacing in the early twentieth century as a weekend getaway/ski resort for foreigners doing business through the Russian rail hub at Harbin.

Yuquanjiu 50 Year
玉 泉 酒 五 十 年 陈 酿
Mixed Aroma
50% ABV
Ingredients: Sorghum

A similar flavour profile to the
Hexie Qingya, only more so. It has
a pungent nose, much stronger
fermented flavours and a hotter
finish.

The story picks up in 1959 with the founding of the
Heilongjiang Yuquan Distillery. The factory first sent its distillers
to Maotai to study the art of producing sauce-aroma baijiu,
whose techniques they adapted to the harsher conditions of the
north. Sauce aroma, however, requires substantial investments
of grain and labour, so the factory leaders set out once more to
find alternatives, this time landing in Sichuan to study strong-
aroma baijiu. Having mastered both southwestern techniques,
they invited several baijiu experts to help them advance their
style and the result was the creation of a mixed-aroma baijiu
in 1975 with the mouth of a strong aroma and the lingering
aftertaste of a sauce aroma. The Beijing-based VATS Group
purchased Yuquan in 2008.

Wuxing
五星
Strong Aroma
52% ABV
Ingredients: Sorghum

Wuxing or 'Five Star' is a surprisingly mellow strong aroma with hints of cashew nut and caramel. It is a well-balanced spirit with a medium spicy finish.

Given the tumult of the last two centuries, it is rare to find a Chinese distillery that can mark a direct lineal descent from its origins, but Yushuqian is an exception. Jiang Yanrun pioneered Yushu's spirit style when he started the Juchengfa Distillery in 1812. In 1946, the distillery changed its name to the Yushu County Distillery and sixth-generation distiller Li Yuntang invented the style of qu used in its signature baijiu, Yushuqian. Yushu later adopted pit fermentation techniques and began producing strong-aroma baijiu. In 2009, Beijing-based VATS Group acquired Yushuqian. It is one of Manchuria's largest distilleries with an annual production capacity of 45000 tonnes.

Chaozhi 10 Year
超值 10 年
Strong Aroma
52% ABV
Ingredients: Sorghum

This attractive bottle bears the four cardinal directions on each side with, you guessed it, 'east' in front. Has a pear-like nose, a mild apricot body and a medium, bitter finish.

BAIJIUS

During the first century, the young man who would later become Emperor Guangwu of Han sought refuge from his enemies at Zhanggong. When he celebrated his narrow escape with a drink, he was so enamoured of the local alcohol that he composed a panegyric in its honour and later named it a court wine. Despite its long connection to winemaking, central China's Henan Province lacks the baijiu bona fides of Sichuan, Jiangsu or even Anhui. It has had to build its reputation for exceptional strong aroma entirely on the quality of its products. Among Henan's largest distillers is Zhanggong, a 1951 state-run distillery that went private in 2003. Zhanggong produces its baijiu with locally sourced sorghum, wheat and barley, and has an annual production capacity of more than 50000 tonnes.

Chuanqi Zhenjiu
传奇珍酒
Sauce Aroma
53% ABV
Ingredients: Sorghum

The classic Zhenjiu is a smooth yet complex full-bodied spirit with an aroma of light soy and a lingering finish.

Zhenjiu is the test case that proves the inseparable bond between a baijiu and its environment. In the early 1970s, Party leaders announced their intentions to expand Kweichow Moutai's production capacity. Situated between mountains and water, Moutai's distillery could not expand its own facilities, so the government chose an alternate site in nearby Zunyi. The 'Offsite Experimental Moutai Distillery' copied the original distillery in excruciating detail, going so far as to transplant dust from Moutai Distillery's ceiling beams. Work began in 1975 and the result, ten years later, produced the full body and lingering aftertaste of a classic sauce aroma, but the taste was too distinct to call it Moutai. It was thus christened Zhenjiu or 'Precious Spirit', and remains a more affordable alternative to its sister baijiu.

Workers spread steamed grains to cool at the **Jiuguijiu** Distillery in Hunan Province

HUANGJIUS

黄酒

No discussion of baijiu would be complete without a brief examination of its progenitor. The term huangjiu translates literally as 'yellow wine' and denotes traditional Chinese grain wines (or beers) that range from light amber to dark brown in colour and thin to viscous in texture. The great breadth of the category is due to a dazzling variety of ingredients and qu largely dependent on regional influences.

Most huangjiu is produced in the Yangtze Delta, which includes Shanghai and the provinces of Jiangsu and Zhejiang, where huangjiu far eclipses baijiu in popularity. Foremost among the region's producers is Shaoxing in Zhejiang. Using the waters from Mirror Lake or *Jianhu*, Shaoxing brewers craft a glutinous rice-based huangjiu fermented in unsealed urns by wheat qu cakes or bricks, and medicinal rice qu. The Shaoxing style has many subcategories, but the two most typical are *yuanhong* 元红 and *huadiao* 花雕 (also *jiafan* 加饭), both semi-dry sherry-like wines, the latter made sweeter with the addition of extra rice during the fermentation process. Further south in Fujian and Jiangxi Provinces, a sweeter and darker style of huangjiu is made by fermenting glutinous rice with red rice qu and medicinal qu. In the pockets of northern China where huangjiu remains popular, rice is often replaced with other grains, most notably millet. Huangjiu is never distilled but is sometimes fortified with baijiu.

Prior to the introduction of distillation to China, almost all of the alcohol consumed there was huangjiu. Until the past

Hakka rice wine in Chuxi, Fujian Province

Chengang in nearby Longyan brews its huangjiu from local red rice

Shaoxing, Zhejiang Province, is China's leading producer of huangjiu. The name 'Shaoxing' is used interchangeably with its huangjiu

When producing huangjiu, the grains are fermented with water and qu open stone

Huangjiu jars outside the **Gu Yue Long Shan** Brewery in Shaoxing

century, huangjiu was always considered more refined and sophisticated than baijiu and was widely celebrated by China's scholar-official aristocracy. With baijiu's ascendance, huangjiu has become a lighter, more affordable alternative and its popularity is once again on the upswing. In recent years huangjiu's prodigious growth rate has outstripped even that of the more popular baijiu. It is estimated that huangjiu consumption more than tripled from 130000 cases in 2001 to 450000 in 2011 – more than 3.5 billion litres.

This brief introduction to huangjiu is by no means exhaustive – entire books are devoted to the subject – but rather an overview of China's best-known huangjiu breweries. In terms of taste and strength, huangjiu is more obviously approachable foreign drinkers, and readers would do well to round out their ly of Chinese alcohol with a bottle or several of huangjiu.

A worker at **Gu Yue Long Shan** prepares rice for brewing huangjiu

CHENGANG 沉 缸
Longmen, Longyan, Fujian | www.lycgjy.com

Gangganghao
缸 缸 好
Huangjiu
12±2% ABV
Ingredients: Glutinous rice

A semi-sweet huangjiu with a subtle, well-balanced combination of dried fruit, toasted rice and barley on the palate. Intended for everyday consumption.

Chengang is southeastern China's best known huangjiu. Brewed in Longyan, whose population is overwhelmingly Hakka (a distinct cultural subdivision of the Han ethnicity), Chengang derives much inspiration from the Hakka's traditional rice wine, or *mijiu*. Chengang huangjiu is typically high in sweetness but complex in flavour, because it uses two kinds of qu: red rice small qu and a secret-recipe medicinal qu containing thirty-two therapeutic ingredients. Its wines are frequently fortified with the addition of an in-house rice baijiu during the fermentation process, which kills the yeast prematurely, allowing for elevated sugar and alcohol levels.

The name Chengang literally means 'sinking jar', which refers to a phenomenon unique to the brewery's fermentation method. Normally when one ferments rice, the alcoholic liquid

Guike
贵 客
Huangjiu
13% ABV
Ingredients: Glutinous rice

A more expensive semi-dry huangjiu, Guike's smell is reminiscent of sherry, but the complex flavour profile has hints of honey, barley and mild aromatics.

will float to the top of the jar and the rice will sink to the bottom. This is not the case with Chengang. During its fermentation process the rice will sink to the bottom of the jar, but the carbon dioxide produced during fermentation will push the rice back to the top of the jar three times. The best alcohol, the brewery maintains, collects at the bottom of the jar, thus they call it Chengang huangjiu.

Written records celebrating the virtues of Longyan's distinctive huangjiu first appeared during the reign of the Jiaqing Emperor (1796–1820), and are attributed to Xiaochi Village, just a few miles distant from the modern brewery. The Chengang Brewery was established by the state in 1957 and purchased by the Hong Kong Chuang Hong Corporation in 1997. It is a medium-sized producer with an annual production capacity of 5000 tonnes.

GU YUE LONG SHAN 古越龙山
Shaoxing, Zhejiang | www.shaoxingwine.com.cn

**Shaoxing Huadiao
10 Year**
绍兴花雕10年
Huangjiu
≥ *14% ABV*
Ingredients: Glutinous rice

A traditional-style Shaoxing wine, its aroma strongly resembles that of sherry with a touch of plum. Its flavour is light, sweet and slightly sour.

Gu Yue Long Shan is to huangjiu what Kweichow Moutai is to baijiu. Among connoisseurs, it is considered to be the cream of Chinese rice wines. It is one of the few huangjius widely available throughout Asia and overseas. It is also the official huangjiu served at Chinese state dinners and other top-level official events.

Its name translates as 'Ancient Yue Dragon Mountain', hearkening back to Shaoxing's distant past. Before China was unified under Qin Shihuang in 221BC, Shaoxing, then called Kuaiji, was capital of the Yue Kingdom. Though little is known today about Yue wines, one famous tale speaks to their strength. On the eve of the decisive battle with the armies of Wu (modern-day Jiangsu Province), King Goujian of Yue poured his wine into a river and commanded his soldiers to drink. According to

Eighty Time
八〇年代
Huangjiu
9 ± 1% ABV
Ingredients: Glutinous rice

With a Chinese name that means the 1980s, this is a new brand likely intended for a younger generation of consumers. A well-balanced huangjiu with a sweet rice flavour.

the legend, mass intoxication resulted and his grateful subjects delivered the king a rout the next day.

The Shaoxing Brewery was established in 1951 through the consolidation of a handful of local breweries, the oldest of which traced its origins to 1664. The next year its operations were expanded at the personal insistence of Premier Zhou Enlai, whose blessing ensured the success of its newly launched brand: Gu Yue Long Shan. The brewery's name was officially changed to its present form in 1987 and it became a publicly listed company in 1997. Gu Yue Long Shan and its subsidiary brands produce more than 140 000 tonnes of huangjiu each year, making it the nation's largest producer by a comfortable margin.

Jimo Laojiu Dihao
5 Year
即墨老酒帝豪五年
Huangjiu
11.5% ABV
Ingredients: Broomcorn millet

A dark brown huangjiu that smells of molasses and chewing tobacco. Has a strong smoky flavour with notes of wood, nuts and stewed plum.

One of the earliest Chinese drinks to use qu was a millet-based huangjiu from Jimo, Shandong Province. The brew was a popular tipple in the courts of the Qin and Han emperors (221BC–220AD), and first mentioned by its modern name in the Northern Song Dynasty (960–1127). During this period its name was changed from *Jimo Laojiu,* meaning 'unstrained wine', to *Laojiu,* 'old wine'. By the 1930s Jimo had around five hundred huangjiu breweries, but that number dwindled to less than twenty by the 1940s. The government consolidated the remaining shops as the 'Jimo Huangjiu Brewery' in 1950, which was purchased by the Hiking Group in 1998.

In both appearance and taste, Jimo Laojiu resembles an English porter. And coincidentally, *Qingdao* (or Tsingtao) became China's best-known beer producer in the twentieth century.

会稽山 KUAIJISHAN

**Shaoxing Huadiao
12 Year**
绍兴花雕 12 年陈
Huangjiu
≥14% ABV
Ingredients: Glutinous rice

One of Kuaijishan's high-end offerings, it has a yeasty aroma that recalls sourdough bread. Its body is thick and viscous, with a tart citrusy flavour similar to sour grapes.

HUANGJIUS

On the outskirts of old Shaoxing sits Kuaiji Mountain (*Shan*), burial place of the semi-mythical Xia Dynasty founder, Yu the Great (c.2200–2100BC). According to legend, Yu's subject Yi Di brewed China's first grain wine. When Yu tasted it, he enjoyed it so much that he promptly outlawed alcohol, fearing the potential political fallout of overindulgence. In a delicious historical irony, his remains were interred in what would become the centre of the huangjiu universe.

Kuaijishan traces its origins to the Yunji Brewery, founded in 1743 along the upper reaches of the Mirror Lake waterways. The brewery was absorbed by the state in 1951, renamed Shaoxing Dongfeng in 1967 and ultimately Kuaijishan in 2005. It is China's second-largest Shaoxing huangjiu producer by volume with an annual output of 10 million litres.

COCKTAILS

EL PRESIDENTE

Ingredients
25ml strong-aroma baijiu
1 fresh pineapple (giving 60ml juice)
20ml cherry brandy
10ml fresh lime juice
10ml syrup of raspberry, strawberry or other red berry
   (1:1 syrup) or grenadine

Instructions
Crush and muddle the pineapple, add the other ingredients and
shake hard over ice. Strain into a chilled glass and garnish with
a cherry and pineapple sail.

Created by: Paul Mathew, The Hide Bar, London, United Kingdom. Originally
prepared with: Shui Jing Fang Wellbay

THE YELLOW EMPEROR

Ingredients
50ml light-aroma baijiu
½ fresh passionfruit
20ml fresh lemon juice
15ml cherry brandy
10ml simple syrup (adjust to taste)

Instructions
Combine all ingredients and shake hard over ice. Fine strain into a chilled champagne saucer.

Created by: Paul Mathew, The Hide Bar, London, United Kingdom.
Originally prepared with: Beijing Erguotou

Chinese Zombie

Ingredients

10ml light-aroma baijiu

30ml rum, infused with candied
  red date

15ml gold rum

15ml dark rum

20ml almond liqueur

60ml pineapple juice

Instructions

Mix all ingredients except baijiu
in a shaker. Shake and strain into
a tiki mug or highball glass. Warm
the baijiu, ignite and pour the
burning spirit into the drink.

Created by: Vance Yeang, Yuan Bar,
Shanghai. Originally prepared with:
Hong Xing Erguotou

COCKTAILS

Fire And Ice

Ingredients

45ml rice-aroma baijiu

2 pickled Thai chillies (muddled
  into baijiu)

½ grapefruit, juiced

Agave nectar to taste

Instructions

Shake all ingredients and serve in
a cocktail glass.

Created by: Robbie Wilson, SNUGbar,
Corvallis, Oregon, USA. Originally
prepared with: Vinn Baijiu

GLOSSARY

ABV (酒精度): Alcohol by volume; a drink's relative ethanol level.

Aging (陈酿;储存;贮存): The process of storing an alcohol for several months or years, allowing it to interact with its surrounding environment. Aging can reduce an alcohol's bitterness and develop its flavours and aromas.

Baijiu (白酒): Any distilled spirit produced in the traditional Chinese style; the subject of this book.

Blending (勾兑;调酒): The process of mixing various distillates together, sometimes with water or neutral spirits, to achieve a desired flavour profile and strength.

Bottling (瓶装): The process of putting a finished alcohol in a bottle.

Brewing (酿酒): The art of creating grain alcohol.

Condenser (冷却器): The part of a still that cools alcoholic vapour back into a liquid; usually consists of a winding tube set inside a bath of cold water.

Continuous mash (续糟): A mash that contains spent mash (previously fermented mash) mixed with fresh grains, similar to the sour mash used in whisky production. This process can raise the mash's acidity and ensure continuity of flavour with previous batches.

Cooling (摊凉): The process of spreading out steamed grains on the cooling ground (凉堂). If the grains are not cooled after steaming, their temperature will kill yeasts and other microorganisms in the qu.

Distillate (蒸馏酒): The liquid produced by distillation; also called distilled alcohol, liquor, spirits, hooch, firewater, et al.

Distillation (蒸馏;烧酒): The process of heating alcohol into vapour and cooling the vapour back into a liquid, reducing water levels and creating a more potent alcohol called a liquor or spirit.

Erguotou (二锅头): Literally 'second pot head', an inexpensive type of light-aroma baijiu normally associated with northeastern China, specifically Beijing.

Ethanol (乙醇): Drinking alcohol, commonly just called alcohol.

Fenjiu (汾酒): A style of light-aroma baijiu originally produced in Fenyang (formerly Fenzhou), Shanxi Province, most closely associated with Xinghuacun Village.

Fermentation (发酵): The chemical interaction between the single-celled organism called yeast and a sugar, which results in the production of carbon dioxide and alcohol. The source of all alcoholic beverages, as well as many foods.

Fermentation jar (酒缸): A jar in which grains are fermented, most commonly associated with light-aroma and rice-aroma baijius, as well as huangjiu.

Fermentation pit (窖池): A pit, usually lined with mud or bricks, in which grains are fermented, most commonly associated with strong-aroma and sauce-aroma baijius.

Gaoliang (高粱): The Chinese word for sorghum, and the name commonly used to denote a style of light-aroma baijiu most popular in Taiwan. Sometimes *kaoliang, kaoliang chiew or gaoliang jiu.*

Ganbei (干杯): Traditional Chinese toast meaning 'dry the glass', 'slam it' or 'bottoms up'; also the act of drinking the entire contents of an alcohol glass in one swig.

Gelatinisation (糊化): The molecular process by which water and heat break down starches into a viscous paste.

Head (酒头): The earliest part of the distillate to come out of the still, typically discarded.

Heart (酒心): The second part of the distillate to come out of the still, typically what will comprise the bulk of the finished liquor.

Huangjiu (黄酒): An undistilled grain alcohol produced according to traditional Chinese methods. Translates as 'yellow wine', but is usually a dark amber colour and can sometimes be closer to transparent.

Husks (稻壳;谷壳): The outer layer of certain grains, often used as filler or insulation in baijiu production.

Infusion (泡酒): A drink created by steeping herbs, spices, fruits or medicine in baijiu or huangjiu.

Mash (酒醅;酒糟): Alcoholic fermenting grains, the prerequisite for producing a distilled spirit. In China, mash is further specified as undistilled mash (酒醅) or spent mash (酒糟).

***Mijiu* (米酒):** A light, transparent huangjiu made from fermented rice, most popular in southeastern China. Also sometimes used as a term to denote rice-aroma baijiu.

Mixed grain (杂粮): A style of strong-aroma baijiu characterised by the use of a multi-grain mash, typically consisting of sorghum, rice, glutinous rice, wheat and corn.

Neutral spirit (酒精): Unflavoured alcohol produced in a column still; ethanol.

Piling (堆积): The process of forming moist grains and qu into piles to trigger saccharification and fermentation before loading the resulting mash into fermentation pits. Piling is most common in the production of sauce-aroma and sesame-aroma baijius.

Qu (曲): The saccharification and fermentation agent used to create traditional Chinese alcohol. The principal qu varieties are big qu, usually made from a combination of wheat, barley and peas, and small qu, made from rice.

Saccharification (糖化): The chemical process of breaking down starch into sugar. A prerequisite of grain fermentation.

'Seas of alcohol' (酒海): A large aging vessel made from a woven basket lined with a paper plaster, most commonly associated with phoenix-aroma baijiu.

Simple grain (单粮): A style of strong-aroma baijiu characterised by the use of an exclusively sorghum mash.

Solid-state distillation (固态发酵): The process of distilling a mash in a mostly solid form by passing steam through it.

Solid-state fermentation (固态蒸馏): The process of fermenting grains in a solid form, rather than steeping saccharified grains to create a sugary broth, or wort, and fermenting the wort into a beer. All traditional Chinese grain alcohols are brewed using solid-state fermentation.

Sorghum (高粱): A tall, stalky grain whose kernels are high in starch and protein. The primary grain used to create most baijiu.

Steamer (甑子;甑桶): The part of a traditional Chinese pot still into which grains and mash are loaded to be steamed and distilled, sometimes at the same time. Consists of a large lidded pot with a grated base set over boiling water.

Steaming (蒸): The process of running steam through grains to help break down their starches and proteins.

Still (蒸馏器): A device used to perform distillation. Most baijiu is produced using a traditional Chinese pot still with a steamer and a condenser, but some rice-aroma baijiu is produced using a continuous still, also called a column still, patent still or Coffey still.

Tail (酒尾): The final part of the distillate to come out of the still, typically discarded, distilled a second time or poured onto mash.

Tonne (吨): The standard measurement of baijiu production, roughly equivalent to 1000 litres or 264 gallons.

TCM (中药): Traditional Chinese medicine, often incorporated into the recipes of rice-based small qu.

Yuanjiu (原酒): Literally 'original alcohol', this is raw distillate that has not yet been aged, diluted or blended.

INGREDIENTS (原料)

Barley (大麦)
Big qu (大曲)
Bran qu (麸曲)
Corn (玉米)
Glutinous rice (糯米)
Millet (小米; 秫;黍;稗)
Rice (大米)
Rice flour (米粉)
Sorghum (高粱)
Small qu (小曲)
Sticky sorghum (糯高粱)
Water (水)
Wheat (小麦)

BIBLIOGRAPHY

Allen, Clement Francis Romilly (trans). *The Book of Chinese Poetry*. London: Kegan Paul, French, Trübner & Co, 1891.

Ang, Kristiano. 'Is the World Ready for Baijiu?' *The Wall Street Journal Scene Asia* (online: http://blogs.wsj.com/scene/2011/08/12/is-the-world-ready-for-baijiu/), 12 Aug 2011.

Baijiu's Boom Times Continue as 1930s Vintage Sells for $409 000 in Beijing.' *Jing Daily*, 1 Jul 2011.

Benson, Charlie. 'Acquiring the Taste.' *The Spirits Business*, 24 Sept 2011.

Bishop, Bill. 'Xi Jiu, a Baijiu Bet on Xi Jinping.' *Sinocism* (online: http://sinocism.com/?p=5036), 3 June 2012.

Bittman, Mark (excerpt by Andrew Kligerman). 'Why Europeans Drank Beer and Asians Drank Tea.' *The New York Times, Diner's Journal* (online: http://dinersjournal.blogs.nytimes.com/2008/07/11/why-europeans-drank-beer-and-asians-drank-tea/), 11 July 2008.

Browne, Frank. 'Samshu.' *Pharmaceutical Journal* 61, July–Dec 1898.

'China: Moët Hennessy Takes Control of Wen Jun Distillery.' *just-drinks* (online: http://www.just-drinks.com/news/mo%C3%ABt-hennessy-takes-control-of-wen-jun-distillery_id90320.aspx), 17 May 2007.

'Chinese Alcohol, Chinese Spirits.' *China Daily*, 27 Oct 2010.

The Chinese Repository X, Jan–Dec 1841.

'Chinese Whispers on Baijiu.' *Drinks International*, 27 Aug 2008.

Cooper, Arthur R.V. (ed.). *Li Po and Tu Fu*. New York: Penguin, 1973.

Craughwell, Thomas J. *The Rise and Fall of the Second Largest Empire in History: How Genghis Khan's Mongols Almost Conquered the World*. Beverly: Fair Winds, 2010.

'China: The IWSR's Annual Report on Consumption of Alcoholic Drinks.' London: International Wine & Spirit Research, May 2012.

Davis, Albert Richard (ed.). *The Penguin Book of Chinese Verse*. New York: Penguin, 1970.

Dickie, Mure and Jones, Adam. 'LVMH Soaks Up Wenjun Stake.' *Financial Times*, 17 May 2007.

'Discovery of Ancient Brewery Dates China's Spirit-making Back 800 Years.' *People's Daily*, 26 Nov 2002.

Downing, C. Toogood. *The Stranger in China; or, the Fan-Qui's Visit to the Celestial Empire, in 1836-7* (Vol. I). Philadelphia: Lea & Blanchard, 1838.

Dudgeon, John. *The Beverages of the Chinese*. Tianjin: The Tientsin Press, 1895.

Duff, Philip. 'Going Against the Grain: Grains, Distilling & Grain Spirits.' (Speech presented at Copenhagen Spirits and Cocktails, Copenhagen, Denmark 25 Feb. 2012. Accessed online: http://www.slideshare. net/philipduff/going-against-the-grain-grains-distilling-grain-spirit.)

Eijkhoff, Pieter. *Wine in China* (unpublished). Utrecht, 2000.

Ember, Melvin, Ember, Carol R., and Skoggard, Ian A. *Encyclopedia of Diasporas: Immigrant and Refugee Cultures around the World* (ebook). New York: Springer, 2004.

Emler, Ron. 'Companies Coy over Chinese Gains.' *The Drinks Business*, 4 Nov 2011.

Evans, Judith. 'Fiery Chinese Drink Challenges West.' *Agence France-Presse*, 19 Oct 2011.

Fairbank, John King and Merle Goldman. *China: A New History*. Cambridge: The Belknap Press of Harvard University Press, 2006.

Fu Jianwei (trans. by Orientaltrans). *Intoxicated in the Land of Wine*. Beijing: China Publishing Group, 2009.

Fu Yuhua, Florentin Smarandache and V. Christianto. *Cultural Advantages in China: Tale of Six Cities*. Infolearnquest, 2009.

'Ganbei! Demand for High-End Spirits Buoys Chinese Producers.' *Jing Daily*, 30 Oct 2012.

Gargan, Edward A. 'China's Heady and Heralded Yellow Wine from Shaoxing.' *The New York Times*, 31 Aug., 1988.

Gately, Iain. *Drink: A Cultural History of Alcohol*. New York: Gotham Books, 2008.

Legge, James (trans). *The Sacred Books of China (Part IV, The Li Ki)*. Oxford: Clarendon Press, 1885.

Li Zhengping. *Chinese Wine*. Cambridge: Cambridge University Press, 2011.

Lin, Lillian. 'Kinmen Legacy Shaped Largely by Efforts of Gen. Hu Lien.' *Central News Agency*, 25 Mar 2010.

Lucas, Louise. 'Diageo's Hopes Rise over Baijiu Move.' *Financial Times*, 2 Mar. 2011.

'LVMH Rebrands Chinese Wenjun Liquor.' *Want China Times*. 25 Mar 2012.

'Kinmen Kaoliang Liquor.' YouTube video (online: http://www.youtube.com/watch?v=SF1FXvuPUzU), posted by culturetw 2 Apr. 2010.

Maclean, Charles (ed.). *Whisky*. New York: Dorling Kindersley, 2008.

MacMillan, Margaret. 'Don't Drink the Mao-Tai.' *Washingtonian*, 1 Feb 2007.

MacMillan, Margaret. *Nixon and Mao: The Week That Changed the World*. New York: Random House, 2007.

Mathew, Paul. 'Chinese Baijiu.' *Blood & Sand* (online: http://www.bloodandsand.com/index.php/chinese-baijiu/), viewed Dec 2011.

Matthews, Erik. 'Aging Gracefully.' *WineMaker*, Winter 2001.

McDonald, Mark. 'One Chinese Liquor Brand Is the Life of the Party.' *International Herald Tribune Rendezvous* (online: http://rendezvous.blogs.nytimes.com/2012/07/03/one-chinese-liquor-brand-is-the-life-of-the-party/), 3 July 2012.

McGovern, Patrick E. *Uncorking the Past: The Quest for Wine, Beer, and Other Alcoholic Beverages*. Berkeley: University of California Press, 2009.

McGovern, Patrick E., Anne P. Underhill, Hui Fang, Fengshi Luan, Gretchen R. Hall, Haiguang Yu, Chen-Shan Wang, Fengshu Cai, Zhijun Zhao, and Gary M. Feinman. 'Chemical Identification and Cultural Implications of a Mixed Fermented Beverage from Late Prehistoric China.' *Asian Perspectives* 44: 249–75, 2004.

McGovern, Patrick E., Juzhong Zhang, Jigen Tang, Zhiqing Zhang, Gretchen R. Hall, Robert A. Moreau, Alberto Nunez, Eric D. Butrym, Michael P. Richards, Chen-shan Wang, Guangsheng Cheng, Zhijun Zhao, and Changsui Wang. 'Fermented Beverages of Pre- and Proto-historic China.' *Proceedings of the National Academy of Sciences USA* 101, 51: 17593–98. 2004.

Mike. 'Mei Jiu Di Tu' 美酒地图. *Zui Shang Gongfu* 嘴上功夫, 门山
2013.

'A "Moonshine" Still in China.' *The World's Advance* 30, No. 4, Apr
1915.

Moutai: Globalization of a Chinese Icon. 2012: Kweichow Moutai.

Munsell, Charles E. 'Analysis of Sam-shu, a Chinese Liquor.' *Journal of
the American Chemical Society* 7. New York: John Polhemus, 1885.

'*Niu Lan Shan Jiu Chang 2012 Nian Chan Liang 6.69 Wan Dun.*' 牛栏
山酒厂2012年产量6.69万吨. *Laodong Wubao* 劳动午报, 9 May 2013.

Owen, Sri. *The Rice Book.* New York: St. Martin's Press, 1993.

Polo, Marco (trans. by Marsden, William). *The Travels of Marco Polo.*
New York: Barnes & Noble Publishing, 2005.

'Pouring a Big One.' *China Economic Review*, 1 May 2008.

Rainey, Lee Dian. *Confucius and Confucianism: The Essentials.*
Malaysia: John Wiley & Sons, 2010.

Ruan, Victoria. 'China to Ban Public Purchases of "High-End" Alcohol.'
Bloomberg Businessweek, 27 Mar 2012.

Shen, Andrew. 'Reality Check: The Chinese Government Spends as
Much on Alcohol as National Defense.' *Business Insider* (online: http://
www.businessinsider.com/china-spends-three-times-more-on-drinking-
than-national-defense-2011-11), 16 Nov 2011.

'*Shun Xin Bai Jiu Ying Shou Yu Da 20 Yi Niu Lan Shan Gan Chao Hong
Xing Er Guo Tou.*' 顺鑫白酒营收预达20亿牛栏山赶超红星二锅头.
Dongfang Zaobao 东方早报, 20 Dec 2011.

'Sichuan Wenjun Spirits Sales Company's Allan Hong on LVMH's Entry
into the Chinese Liquor Market.' YouTube video (online: http://www.
youtube.com/watch?v=6oPp42Gpahw), posted by INSEADofficial,
26 Aug 2012.

Smith, C. Wayne and Richard A. Frederiksen (eds.). *Sorghum: Origin,
History, Technology, and Production.* New York: John Wiley & Sons,
2000.

Sonne, Paul and Laurie Burkitt. 'China Approves Diageo Baijiu Bid.'
The Wall Street Journal, 27 June 2011.

'Sweet Sorghum in China.' *Agriculture and Consumer Protection Department Food and Agriculture Organization of the United Nations*, Feb 2002.

Tan, Clement and John Ruwitch. 'China's Downturn-Proof Booze Makers Hit Government Wall.' *Reuters*, 10 Aug 2012.

'Top Ten Gifts for the Chinese Luxury Consumer 2012.' *Hurun Report*, 11 Jan 2012.

Uchibayashi, Masao. 'Maize in Pre-Columbian China.' *Journal of the Pharmaceutical Society of Japan* 125:7 (2005).

Waddell, Helen (trans.). *Lyrics from the Chinese*. New York: Houghton Mifflin, 1913.

Waley, Arthur (trans.). *A Hundred and Seventy Chinese Poems*. New York: Alfred A. Knopf, 1919.

Waley, Arthur (trans.). *More Translations from the Chinese*. New York: Alfred A. Knopf, 1919.

Wang Guochun 王国春 (ed.). *Bai Nian Zhui Qiu Bai Nian Fen Jin*. 百年追求百年奋进. Chengdu: Wuliangye 五粮液, 2009.

Wang Kai 王恺 (ed.). *San Lian Sheng Huo Zhou Kan* 三联生活周刊 675 (26 Mar 2012).

Weems, J.B. 'Chemistry of Clays.' *Iowa Geological Survey Annual Report* 14 (1903).

'Will Baijiu Ever Become Fashionable?' *Jing Daily*, 25 May 2010.

World Health Organization. 'Global Status Report on Alcohol and Health.' Geneva: WHO Press, 2011.

Xie Yu. 'Ban Moutai at Official Banquets, Says Deputy.' *China Daily*, 17 Jan 2012.

Xu Ganrong and Bao Tongfa. *Grandiose Survey of Chinese Alcoholic Drinks and Beverages* (中国酒大观目录, Chinese and English versions). Jiangnan University (online: http://www.sytu.edu.cn/zhgjiu/jmain.htm), 1998.

Xu Yuanzhong (trans.). *300 Tang Poems*. Beijing: China Translation Export Co., 1987.

Yang Chen (ed.). *Lu Zhou Lao Jiao: Zhong Guo Rong Yao* 泸州老窖: 中国荣耀. Chengdu: Qiyuan Zhiban 启源制版, 2010.

Zhang Wenxue 张文学 and Xie Ming 谢明 (ed.). *Zhong Guo Jiu Ji Jiu Wen Hua Gai Lu* 中国酒及酒文化概论. Chengdu: Sichuan Daxue Chuban She 四川大学出版社, 2010.

Zhang Xiaoyang 张销样 (ed.). *Wu Qian Nian Zhong Hua Wen Ming Xi Feng Jiu Wen Hua* 五千年中华文明西凤酒文化. Beijing: Zhongguo Xiju Chuban She 中国戏剧出版社, 2007.

Zhang Yi, He Yue, and Zhou Changqing. 'Nation's Oldest Brewery Unearthed in Northeast China.' *Xinhua*, 14 May 2012.

PHOTO CREDITS

All photographs in this book are copyright Derek Sandhaus except where indicated below.

500 Spirits International: 68

Byejoe: 75, 76

Diageo: 50, 65

Getty/John Dominis: 20–21

Guilin Sanhua Co., Ltd.: 40

Hetrick, Todd: 10, 25 (*top*), 58 (*bottom*), 163 (*upper left and middle*)

iStock/CaoChunhai: 62

iStock/YinYang: 160–61

Jiugui Liquor Co., Ltd.: 18, 159

Kweichow Moutai Co., Ltd.: *Titles*, 36, 41, 42, 43, 44, 46, 56

Kouzijiuye: 101

Liu, Imogen: 25, 34

Luzhou Laojiao I&E Co., Ltd.: 65 (*bottom*)

Mathew, Paul: 172, 174

Project Spirits, LLC.: 117

Simak, Evelyn: 26 (*right*)

Vinn Distillery: 138, 175 (*top*)

Wuliangye Group I and E Co., Ltd.: 16–17, 37 (*middle right*)

Yili Xiaoerbulake Jiuye Co., Ltd.: 38

Yuan: 61, 175 (*bottom*)

Zhejiang Gu Yue Long Shan Shaoxing Wine Co., Ltd.: 23 (*top*), 164, 165

ACKNOWLEDGMENTS

This book is the culmination of an intense period marked by stacks of baffling Chinese source material and seemingly endless shots of baijiu. That I lived to tell the tale and formulate my thoughts into a relatively sober exploration of Chinese spirits is a testament not to any supernatural ability on my part, but rather to the boundless generosity of friends and strangers.

First, I would like to thank every baijiu and huangjiu producer who contributed bottles, images or otherwise advanced my understanding of Chinese alcohol. You made me feel welcome in your homes, and I hope your drinks will be likewise welcomed abroad.

For their assistance with research and translations, I owe a great debt to Duan Li and Lü Jing. Your company and instruction were a bright spot in a gray city. And thanks to Grace Jiang, who tirelessly hunted down the bulk of the bottles featured in this collection. This book would have hardly been possible without all of your help.

Creating tasting notes for baijiu like those featured in this collection required the palates of many thoughtful drinkers. All of their feedback was considered and incorporated into the descriptions that are found in these pages, so each taster played an integral role. I would thus like to thank the guests of my Shanghai tasting: Jeannie Cho Lee MW, Jim Boyce, Justin Fischer, Seamus Harris, Dan Bignold, Alexander Barlow, Tiffany 'Madame Moutai' Yang and Ying Guo. An additional nod is owed to Dan and the rest of the team at *DRiNK* magazine for their tactical support and Steffy Zhu, owner of the exquisite Yuan Bar, for hosting the event. I would also like to thank my Chengdu tasters: Alexander Cohen, Pope Thrower and Sherry Huang, as well as Kim Dallas, Catherine Platt, Peter Goff, Andrew Barnett and the entire staff of the Chengdu Bookworm, who organised the most fraught of the tastings.

I am also indebted to those who stood by me through many a memorable *ganbei*. Todd Hetrick, Johan Simonson, Walter Kerr, Eitan Plasse, Dan Cohn, Abo, Xiao Li, Pete Sweeney and Andrew Galbraith – the next round is on me. And Alex, you deserve a separate mention for how much I made you put away.

Perhaps most importantly, I would like to thank my editors Mike Tsang and Imogen Liu, as well as my designer Steffan Leyshon-Jones. Thanks also to Jo Lusby and the other fine people at Penguin China who made this book happen. And to Paul French for bringing us together.

Finally, I would like to thank Catherine for her support and inexhaustible well of patience. I will never make you drink another shot.

INDEX

BAIJIU: THE ESSENTIAL GUIDE TO CHINESE SPIRITS

INDEX